Forthcoming Volumes in the New
Church's Teaching Series

The Anglican Vision
James E. Griffiss

Opening the Bible
Roger Ferlo

Engaging the Word
Michael Johnston

The Practice of Prayer
Margaret Guenther

Living with History
Fredrica Harris Thompsett

Early Christian Traditions
Rebecca Lyman

Opening the Prayer Book
Jeffrey Lee

Mysteries of Faith
Mark McIntosh

Ethics After Easter
Stephen Holmgren

Christian Social Witness
Harold Lewis

Horizons of Mission
Titus L. Presler

A Theology of Worship
Louis Weil

Mysteries of Faith

The New
Church's Teaching Series,
Volume 8

Mysteries
of
Faith

Mark McIntosh

A COWLEY PUBLICATIONS BOOK

Lanham, Chicago, New York, Toronto, and Plymouth, UK

A Cowley Publications Book
Published by Rowman & Littlefield Publishers, Inc.
A wholly owned subsidiary of
The Rowman & Littlefield Publishing Group, Inc.
4501 Forbes Boulevard, Suite 200, Lanham, Maryland 20706
http://www.rowmanlittlefield.com

Estover Road, Plymouth PL6 7PY, United Kingdom

The title *The Church's Teaching Series* is used by permission of the Domestic and Foreign Missionary Society. Use of the series title does not constitute the Society's endorsement of the content of the work.

Cover art: *The Annunciation*, early 14th century (Byzantine)

Scripture quotations are taken from *The New Revised Standard Version* of the Bible, © 1989, by the Division of Christian Education of the national Council of the Churches of Christ in the United States of America. Used by permission.

British Library Cataloguing in Publication Information Available

Library of Congress Cataloging-in-Publication Data
McIntosh, Mark Allen, 1960–
    Mysteries of Faith / Mark McIntosh.
        p. cm. — (The new church's teaching series; v. 8)
    Includes bibliographical references.
    ISBN 978-1-56101-175-9 (alk. Paper)
    1. Theology, Doctrinal—Popular works. I. Title. II. Series.
BT77.M386 2000
230—dc21   99-046467

♾^{TM} The paper used in this publication meets the minimum requirements of American National Standard for Information Sciences—Permanence of Paper for Printed Library Materials, ANSI/NISO Z39.48-1992.
Printed in the United States of America

Table of Contents

The New Church's Teaching Series

Almost fifty years ago a series for the Episcopal Church called The Church's Teaching was launched with the publication of Robert Dentan's *The Holy Scriptures* in 1949. Again in the 1970s the church commissioned another church's teaching series for the next generation of Anglicans. Originally the series was part of an effort to give the growing postwar churches a sense of Anglican identity: what Anglicans share with the larger Christian community and what makes them distinctive within it. During that seemingly more tranquil era it may have been easier to reach a consensus and to speak authoritatively. Now, at the end of the twentieth century, consensus and authority are more difficult; there is considerably more diversity of belief and practice within the churches today, and more people than ever who have never been introduced to the church at all.

The books in this new teaching series for the Episcopal Church attempt to encourage and respond to the times and to the challenges that will usher out the old century and bring in the new. This new series differs from the previous two in significant ways: it has no official status, claims no special authority, speaks in a personal voice, and comes not out of committees but from scholars and pastors meeting and talking informally together. It assumes a different readership: adults who are not "cradle Anglicans," but who come from other religious traditions or from no tradition at all, and who want to know what Anglicanism has to offer.

As the series editor I want to thank E. Allen Kelley, former president of Morehouse Publishing, for initially inviting me to bring together a group of teachers and pastors who could write with learning and conviction about their faith. I am grateful both to him and to Morehouse for participating in the early development of the series.

Since those initial conversations there have been changes in the series itself, but its basic purpose has remained: to explore the themes of the Christian life through Holy Scripture, historical and contemporary theology, worship, spirituality, and social witness. It is our hope that all readers, Anglicans and otherwise, will find the books an aid in their continuing growth into Christ.

James E. Griffiss
Series Editor

Acknowledgments

That great Anglican priest and poet George Herbert once wrote that prayer is:

Church-bels beyond the starres heard,
the souls bloud
The land of spices; something understood.

If prayer is "something understood," theology is the struggle to put what has been understood in prayer into words. In the history of Christianity it is a comparatively recent idea to think of theology as solely a matter of arguments and propositions. Those have always been important elements of theology, but equally so the visionary insight of martyrs, the compassionate understanding of saints, and the contemplative wisdom of all who give themselves to a life of service and prayer. Theology, I believe, is a sharing in the mystery of God's life; it is what happens as God the Holy Spirit works within us the mystery of the Father's Word made flesh. And it is, I believe, a deeply Anglican intuition to draw our theology from our life of common prayer throughout the ages.

My deepest gratitude goes to all whose teaching exemplifies this integrity of theology and prayer in the theological mission of the church; their work has inspired this book. Especially in this regard I am truly indebted and thankful to bishops Frank Griswold and Rowan Williams; to Canon James Griffiss, who also labored long over my torturous drafts with much wisdom.

I also owe great thanks to Cynthia Shattuck and Vicki Black of Cowley Publications, who persevered in the cause of clarity and readability throughout; and also to my former graduate assistant at Loyola, Bryan Hall, who greatly assisted me.

I am grateful to the many lay and clergy gatherings who have listened to the book's ideas and helped me to work them out, especially Robert and Laurel Warski of the Episcopal Church of the Redeemer in Elgin, Illinois, who commented on many chapter drafts. I am also grateful to Father Randall Haycock, Deacon Mary Harriss, and all the members of that parish whose life of service, devotion, and worship was the context of my writing.

Finally, I am as ever so thankful to my dear family, especially Anne, and our children, Liza and Nathan, and to my brothers and sister. This book is dedicated lovingly to those who have taught me much about living life together: to my father- and mother-in-law, Frederick and Elizabeth Nagle, and to my own mother, Katherine, and to the memory of my father, Gilbert McIntosh.

Chapter One

Mysteries of Faith

Let the same mind be in you that was in Christ
Jesus.

Philippians 2:5

This is a book about theology. I hope it will entice
you to do theology yourself—or to discover how
much theology you already do. So this is not a book
about theology in the sense of telling you what pro-
fessional theologians have said. It is more us exploring
together what doing theology is like, and seeing what
we see.

I remember the first time I looked into the Grand
Canyon. It was unbelievably vast and beautiful. The
sheer aching space seemed alive, echoing, ringing with
an immense majesty. But I also remember being
astonished at how easily it vanished: when I stepped
back just a few feet from the edge of the canyon, I was
completely unaware that this huge reality was right
before me. Theology is walking up to the edge and
noticing the mystery before you.

I say theology deals in mystery because most of
what it ponders is not a "thing" that can be seen. A
poor woman cradling a child in a stable is something
we can see; the meaning of it is not so apparent. A Jew
being put to death by the Romans is something we can

see; the meaning of it passes understanding. So theology is all about sidling up to these mysteries of faith and peering into their depths. I do not mean "mystery" in the sense of an intricate puzzle or problem to be solved. I mean "mystery" as the deep dimension of life where meaning dwells. Most of the time we walk along the surface of things happily enough. But every once in a while there is a bend in the path and we find ourselves at the edge of a vast dimension of meaning, hope, fear, pain, courage, or love. After eighteen years of life together, a marriage fails. Or a new job opens up a whole world of skills and interests that changes our life. Or a child reads a poem at her grandmother's funeral. Or a dragonfly hovers over some roses in late summer light. Mystery is what beckons and speaks to us out of such moments. It is not something *different* from our everyday lives; it is the real *meaning* of our lives, the secret truth of them.

And theology is about seeking out and listening to that meaning, hearing it not just as any kind of meaning but as *God's* meaning. What does it mean for God that a dragonfly hovers or a child reads a poem? What does your life mean as it takes place moment by moment in the presence of God? If there are times when you would like to ask such questions, even to venture an answer, then theology is the tool you want to use.

Of course there are people who do not think there is any meaning to life, or who think that the quest for meaning is a purely private matter. But most of us feel that life does have some kind of meaning, more or less. In the big scheme of things, my toaster has less meaning and less mystery than does, say, the hickory tree under which I used to read as a child. So there is a depth to life, an intensity that opens up a dimension of meaning more easily in some things than in others:

I have always enjoyed toast, but the making of it has simply never been as *meaningful* to me as the memories of childhood.

Moreover, the meaning of things usually depends, we say, not just on private feelings but on a shared context. Giving someone flowers means one thing in the context of an office birthday party, and something rather different in the context of the high school prom. Theology is about seeing the meaning of things in the context of life with God. For example, a meal with your friends means something generally pleasurable in the context of our culture; in the context of life with God such a meal might mean a lot more—especially if the meal becomes an occasion of that deep self-sharing with one another we call communion.

In this chapter I want to offer three ways of thinking about how theology explores mystery, how it listens for the meaning of things by hearing in them and through them and beyond them the life of God. We could say that these are three "moments" or stages in the theological journey; sometimes they happen neatly one after another (and I will take them that way), but quite often they overlap and spiral back again like old friends whose recurring presence in our lives keeps changing and deepening, enriching us with every visit.

∼ The First Moment: Seeing Differently
I have been saying that theology ponders the deep meaning of everyday life by seeing our lives as taking place within God's life. There are certain moments, of course, when we just sense, almost intuitively, that what is happening is terribly significant or somehow holy—moments, in other words, when the mystery of things seems to well up before us and, like Abraham or Jacob, we know that we are in the presence of God.

If you have ever watched the sun set over a silent northern lake with the sky so richly purple and red you could hardly breathe; or if you have ever walked quietly into a tiny child's bedroom at night and watched her rustle gently under her blanket, so that for a moment you ache with the memory of your own distant past; or if you have ever watched and prayed as a young medical intern, gray with fatigue and lack of sleep, worked desperately through the night to save a patient in distress: if you have known any of these things, or a hundred others like them, then you have already begun to theologize.

You have begun to theologize, I think, because moments like these seem to put us at the edge of mystery—like wandering unsuspectingly up to the edge of the Grand Canyon. You cannot help but be in awe. You are drawn quite naturally to wonder about the meaning of it all, to wonder about the hand of God in it. But as we all know, most of life is not quite like that. We can rarely count on something awe-inspiring to awaken us to the fact that (whether we know it or not) we are standing all the time at the edge of mystery, in the presence of God.

Even if you did have such an awakening, so that every moment of life seemed drenched with eternity, so that you began to see God in all things, how would you know what it all meant? For instance, I can visit someone's home and know that almost everything I see is in some way a meaningful part of his life. But if the person I am visiting is a near stranger to me, then the meaning of what I see remains closed and obscure. On the desk is an enormous paperweight—a stone with a crayon drawing pasted rather messily to the top, clearly the work of a child's hands. Why is it there, what meaning does it have? Did he make it himself as a present one Father's Day years ago?

Unless I get to know the story of my host, and something about his character, the meaning of what I see is hard to read. I need to learn the context.

For Christians, the context of the world's life is provided by the story of God's life with the world. The story that opens in paradise and ends in the coming of God's kingdom is the context we need. Our lives take place within this story of God's desire to bring life into being out of nothing, to bring Israel to birth out of slavery in Egypt, to come among us as Jesus and draw us into the divine plan by the outpouring of the Holy Spirit. This is the context in which theology explores the meaning of life. This story of God's life with us is the deep landscape against which we begin to notice and recognize the mystery of love at work in everything.

If you have ever found yourself utterly absorbed in a novel, you will have a sense of what I am trying to describe. I confess that I am an ardent reader of the marvelous sea novels of Patrick O'Brian. Swept along in the wonders of this series, I can (reluctantly) put down a given volume (there are nineteen and counting!) yet see the real world around me with something of the straining hopefulness of Captain Jack Aubrey; I find myself scanning the horizon with a new keenness of attention, congratulating friends on their successes with a newly unself-conscious heartiness, or abandoning myself to the joys of a Boccherini sonata I never knew could be so delightful. But then, alas, the wisps of keenness and kindness and the bold stances of that imaginary world aboard ship begin to fade before the mundane realities of my desktop and our baby's diaper-changing table and the need to get to work on time. And yet when the thought of my friends in O'Brian's great fictional world crosses my mind, my heart lifts, an encouraging chuckle rises to my lips, and I know that my own daily round can be invested with the expectancy and noble wonder I have absorbed from these remarkable tales.

Whether they be O'Brian novels or a favorite movie, or even a story from childhood we have never forgotten, these are the things that shape the way we look at life and give us a context for interpreting what goes on around us. If a fine novel can so animate our thoughts, how much more can a story that is no novelist's lovely fancy but the very truth of life itself reinterpret our entire lives—a story told in the cry of a poor child in a manger and a young Jew dying on a cross. John's gospel speaks of Jesus as God's Word, *Logos* in the original Greek. We could also translate *Logos* as rationale or meaning. The life that Jesus lived, the death he died, the resurrection that he opens before us—this is the divine Meaning, the meaning of life itself, that gives meaning to our lives.

I am suggesting that the story of creation and salvation can become the story by which we see the truth of what is going on in our lives and in our world. We see Jesus himself using little stories—parables—in just this way throughout the gospels. Someone gives him a proper answer about loving God and neighbor, but then asks further, "And who is my neighbor?" (Luke 10:29). How do I know the *meaning* of being a neighbor? And in reply Jesus tells the story of the priest, the Levite, and the good Samaritan who had very different reactions to the man they see robbed, beaten, and left for dead in a ditch. After telling this story Jesus asks, "Which of these three, do you think, was a neighbor to the man who fell into the hands of robbers?" (Luke 10:36). In the stunning and eye-opening world of this parable, being a neighbor turns out to have nothing to do with sharing a religious system or even being a good person, but simply with having compassion at the ready.

Thus in this story Jesus creates a context in which his hearers can begin to perceive the meaning and truth of their own actions. The patterns of disregard or fear on the one hand and self-giving concern on the other are the structures of this parable. These same structures become the patterns by which we see how we ourselves relate to one another. How often I have tiptoed uneasily past a person standing all alone at coffee hour, just because I wanted to get on with more "important" church business at a meeting! Left to my own reading of the situation, I might well say that the meaning of my action was simply an honest concern for getting to the worship committee meeting on time. But if I read my action in the context of the parable of the good Samaritan, then the deep mystery of my own fear and mistrust, my unneighborliness, becomes apparent. And, perhaps if Jesus' story is ingrained deeply enough in my heart, I will feel the tugging of Christ's own compassion for this stranger standing at the edges of our community life.

Any powerful and familiar story can give new and deeper meaning to the lives of those who know the story. But with God's story we are not left to puzzle and ponder over the meaning of the story by ourselves, for the same God who speaks this Word into our midst also pours the Holy Spirit into our hearts. Thus as we are drawn into this great story we discover that our lives have been taking place within this context all along, without our even realizing it. God the Holy Spirit opens our hearts to perceive the truth taking place in our lives. It is a disturbing and exhilarating process: where before things were reasonably manageable, now we begin to sense the eternal significance of our choices. Before we were simply going to

avoid the co-worker whose behavior seemed to suggest an addiction problem; now we begin wonder
what it means to be that person's neighbor, what it
means that Christ died for that person, what it means
that we seem to be noticing that person's problems in
a new way.

Theology is taking place whenever your life is
interpreted in the context of God's life, when the mystery of God's love begins to shine and radiate into
your world, illuminating its meaning and purpose in
ways both unexpected and life-changing. St. Paul
speaks of it as having the mind of Christ (Philippians
2:5). The very Spirit of Christ comes to renew our
minds, sensitizing them to a whole realm of meaning
whose presence we barely discern within our daily
lives. Sharing the mind of Christ does not make us
oblivious to what is going on around us—just the
opposite. As the Spirit fills the church with the mind
of Christ, and his vision begins to clarify our own, we
find ourselves able to converse with the deep longings
and potentials of all kinds of people around us, appre-
hending something of the vast significance of a simple
act of compassion or an unthinking betrayal.

So the first "moment" in theology is God's Word
speaking a universe into being and calling a people,
Israel, to hear and respond to that Word. Israel's story
with God has made the divine Word audible to us.
God's Word has spoken "in many and various ways"
(Hebrews 1:1), and Christians believe it is spoken
definitively in the life, death, and resurrection of Jesus.
He is that Word, that Meaning, spelled out in the story
of one human life. In Christ, God speaks the context in
which we begin to notice the deep mystery of life.

In the context of modern culture, someone next to
us on the bus may be a benign if unknown quantity;
but in the context of God's story, the person next to us

is a brother or sister for whom Christ died and the bearer, like each one of us, of an immortal destiny. C. S. Lewis spoke arrestingly of this growing awareness that, in God's plan of salvation, everyone we meet is a player in the eternal drama and the stakes of our relations with one another are inestimably great. Everyone's life has a hidden dimension of mystery whose significance we can only glimpse when we see them in the light of God's speaking and acting. If we see the world in terms of God's life, says Lewis, then we have to

> remember that the dullest and most uninterest-ing person you can talk to may one day be a creature which, if you saw it now, you would be strongly tempted to worship, or else a horror and a corruption such as you now meet, if at all, only in a nightmare. All day long we are, in some degree, helping each other to one or other of these destinations. It is in light of these over-whelming possibilities, it is with the awe and circumspection proper to them, that we should conduct all our dealings with one another.... There are no *ordinary* people.[1]

Theology, in other words, is a joyfully serious busi-ness. Its starting point and source is the fact that God has embraced our world within the divine plan. This means that all we do and think takes place against the divine landscape and its meaning emerges in that light. It means that all our lives are invested with an eternal significance because they have, by grace, become significant for God. We are acting in the drama of God's life; that is the story going on in our lives.

And that brings us to the second "moment" in the-ology, which is constantly evoked by the first. The first moment is *God's speaking* of the story that becomes the context of our lives. The second moment is *our hearing* of God's Word, our reception of it as the very meaning of life.

∼ The Second Moment:
Theology as a Habit of Life

Since this second moment of theology seems to be something *we* are supposed to do it is easy to overlook God's role in the process. But the early Christians talked about God's role in our *hearing* of the Word too; they spoke of it as inspiration by the Spirit. The speaking and narrating of the world's story as God's story is the work of the Word, while bringing this divine Word to birth in the life of the church and in our lives as members of the church is the work of the Holy Spirit.

Take the analogy of reading a novel, and the powerful impression the work makes upon you. The words convey the author's ideas, and then go on to reach into your heart and mind, bringing the ideas to life in your own life. It is not just a mechanical process: you do not read a novel and then go and imitate its characters. It is more interior, as though the vision and the meaning of the story came to inspire you, to dwell in you, and gradually to transform your own thinking and acting. In this way, you might say, the meaning of the story comes to birth in your own life. This can happen in even a fairly trivial case: millions of people read a book about climbing Mount Everest, and suddenly the spirit of adventure and the quest for the ultimate comes to dwell in many of them. They have begun to interpret their lives in this context of life-as-quest, and in some cases the patterns and rhythms of their lives will begin to change, to be animated by the power of the story. The meaning and purpose of life is now different, and everything has a new significance.

So too, in a far more wonderful way, this happens in the case of God's story. For the power of God's story and its ability to inspire and reshape our lives is not from the inanimate effect of words. It is the very Spirit of God who comes to dwell within us, giving us ears to hear the Word and tongues to share with others the meaning it has for life. You could even say that God the Holy Spirit confronts us with God's story, makes it alive in us, capable of renewing our hearts and minds, able to conceive the meaning of life in ways past our understanding. In St. Luke's gospel, Mary literally conceives Jesus because, according to the angel Gabriel, "the Holy Spirit will come upon you, and the power of the Most High will overshadow you" (Luke 1:35). The Holy Spirit empowers us to conceive God's Word in our own life, to be Word-bearers to one another.

This is all more than a little overwhelming, because it means that hearing and receiving God's Meaning is not going to be something we can do in a single hour on Sunday morning. The divine Meaning who will give meaning to our lives cannot really be heard that way—like a news broadcast we can flip on for a bit and then switch off without leaving our chair. Hearing and receiving God's Word so that it can reveal the truth of our lives is going to mean a very active kind of listening. It is going to mean that we will only truly hear this Word insofar as it comes to be spoken with the very stuff of our lives. This idea is not unheard of: there are many important qualities, like courage or love, that we can never really "know" in the abstract. Being able to recite the dictionary definition of joy is not really the same as knowing the meaning of joy by being joyful ourselves. So, not surprisingly, knowing the Meaning of the universe is going to involve letting that Meaning take root and grow and unfold in the patterns of our own life.

And that is why we want to talk about this second moment in theology in terms of habit. Learning to see the mystery of God's plan, to see it in a way that illuminates the meaning of the world, requires us to develop some habits of mind and heart. The word "habit" comes from the Latin *habitus*, meaning a condition or character; it is a form of the Latin verb *habere*, meaning to have and to hold. So when theology becomes a habit, it becomes part of your character, a fundamental having and holding of who you are. Or we could say that theology "inhabits" you, that God's Word comes to dwell within your heart by the power of the Spirit.

What would having a theological habit of heart be like? My hunch is that it would not be like knowing certain pieces of information that other people do not know. Rather, it would be more like knowing *how* to do something, like having the *hang* of it. Developing a theological habit of heart would mean being so inhabited by all the mysteries of faith that you have an almost instinctive feel for the deep meaning of every situation in the light of those mysteries; it would mean that reading the world in the light of God's life is like second nature to you. All this points to what is really a life-long process of formation, a process in which, by prayer and worship, service and mission, we are transformed by the Spirit of Christ, and inhabited by his life as the meaning of our lives.

Most of us have met people whose profound personal involvement in all the aspects of their work have made them truly exemplary in their fields. We often say of such people that they seem to "have it in their bones"; they just know the right thing to do or to say in almost any situation. They have acquired discern-ment. That is the kind of deep, personally integrated knowing that the Spirit brings to birth in Christians.

I remember with deep affection and humble grati-tude my meetings as a young seminarian with an Anglican nun, Mother Mary Clare, at one time the superior of a contemplative religious order for women. She knew the scriptures so deeply, had medi-tated so lovingly on all the mysteries of our faith—God as Trinity, the Incarnation, salvation, and so on—that coming to talk with her really did feel to me as though I were coming into the presence of God. She seemed to understand me so completely, to know so perfectly well what I was hiding from, what I needed to ask for, what I needed to hear. Coming to her for spiritual direction was sometimes rather frightening, because I could feel how much God was loving me through Mother Mary Clare, how much and how clearly God was speaking through her the Word who could be a word of life to me. She was always loving and peaceful, and yet also alert, sensitive to any hint of falseness or self-deception in what I said. She read widely and probably understood quantum mechanics, for all I know, but it was not how well-informed she was that gripped me; it was how personally she understood repentance and forgiveness, sacrifice, guilt, fear, faith, hope, and love. God's Word had truly taken flesh in her, and she was able to help me under-stand more clearly the meaning of my life in the con-text of God's plan.

We could contrast such a theological habit of mind and heart with the insensitivity and spiritual clumsi-ness that overtakes us all sometimes. Developing and nourishing a good theological habit takes time, patience, and practice. And we all know how easy it is to fall out of a good habit, especially one that seems to have little reward in the present state of the world. In such a case our habit can atrophy, weaken, or—which is sometimes worse—harden into a brittle imitation of what it used to be. We overhear a warning about the dangers of this kind of spiritual numbness in the letter to the Ephesians:

> You must no longer live as the Gentiles live, in the futility of their minds. They are darkened in their understanding, alienated from the life of God because of their ignorance and hardness of heart. They have lost all sensitivity and have abandoned themselves to licentiousness, greedy to practice every kind of impurity. (Ephesians 4:17-19)

Losing a theological habit of life is like living in a world defined entirely by daytime television talk shows, where everything is reduced to the most abject level of banal hysteria imaginable within nine-minute time segments. On the other hand, being inhabited by the good news of God's life with us is what gives Christians a sense of proportionality and balance, a sense of the true perspective with which to judge things. This habit of discerning the meaning of things in the light of God is, then, the second moment of theology.

∿ The Third Moment:
Theology as Conversation with God

I have said that theology is at heart a life-long journey of growth. It is a journey that God calls us to begin by speaking to us, communicating to us the Word or Meaning of God's life. That is the first stage of the journey. But God does not simply leave the Word "out there," spoken into a world of unhearing passersby. God pours out the Holy Spirit upon the world, and suddenly people begin to hear the Word, to receive it as the very meaning of life, and to see all things in its light. And that is the second stage of the journey. Perhaps the best way to think about what comes next is to say that the habit of theology develops into theology that is a conversation. We see this most clearly in St. Paul's beautiful statement that we have not received the Spirit of fear and slavery, but of adoption into God's life:

> All who are led by the Spirit of God are children of God. For you did not receive a spirit of slavery to fall back into fear, but you have received a spirit of adoption. When we cry, "Abba! Father!" it is that very Spirit bearing witness with our spirit that we are children of God. (Romans 8:14–16)

Let's take a moment to consider this crucial text. Paul is saying that what the Spirit does in us is to draw us into a relationship, a loving relationship into which we are adopted as children of God. This relationship is the relationship between Jesus and his *Abba* or Father. As the Spirit brings Christ's life to birth in our life, we find ourselves sharing with Christ in the most central and characteristic aspect of his life—namely the relationship that defines him and marks him as God's beloved child, his relationship with God as the loving source of his whole life. And more wonderfully yet, we find that we do not remain mute observers of this relationship, but that the Spirit actually teaches us the very language of Jesus' conversation with the Father. The Spirit puts Jesus' words of loving adoration and trust in our own hearts and makes it possible for us to speak them ourselves.

Two things are especially worth noting here. First, this experience of Paul and the early Christians is the basis of our understanding of God as Trinity, as a "conversation" taking place between Jesus and the Father in their Spirit. We will look more closely at this in the next chapter on the mystery of the Trinity. In my own view, the growing recognition within the Christian community that something unbelievable was happening to them marks the birth of Christian theology: the community was being plunged by the Spirit not just into Jesus' life, but into his relationship with the Father. The Spirit who animates Jesus' relationship with the Father is no alien force; the Spirit is God as relationship, as the love who draws Jesus to the Father and the Father to Jesus. And because it is this same God the Holy Spirit who comes to dwell in the church's life, we too are drawn into Jesus' life of relationship with the Father. In fact, we could even say that the Spirit *is* this relationship between the Father and the Son, that the Spirit is the power, the loving energy of the Speaker's speaking of the Word. And this divine speech comes, by the Spirit's power, to break out in our life as church at Pentecost.

The second thing to notice is equally remarkable. Not only are we invited into the conversation, but we turn out to be, in our own inimitably recalcitrant but cherishable way, part of the very subject matter of the conversation. We are what God is talking about. When Jesus prays to the Father, he prays about his work with us, about his disciples and all who will be drawn through our feeble witness into God's family:

> I ask not only on behalf of these, but also on behalf of those who will believe in me through their word, that they may all be one. As you, Father, are in me and I am in you, may they also be in us. (John 17:20-21)

As the church has reflected on and lived within the reality of which this and similar passages speak, we have begun, faintly and very imperfectly, to hear and understand the infinite scope of this conversation, this prayer, this life being shared by the Father and the Son. Gradually Christians have begun to sense that the matter and substance of God's conversation involves not only us, but the whole universe. Everything that is has been spoken into existence by God; the universe is an event, a phrase, in the language of the Speaker's speaking, and the Word's expression of divine Meaning, and the Spirit's loving of that infinitely self-giving conversation.

Have you ever traveled in another country where you did not speak the language? All around you can hear people laughing and talking, making jokes, arguing, scolding, forgiving, giving directions. The sheer impenetrability of all that speech can become tiring, even frustrating. There is so much going on you would like to understand, to take part in! But if you persevere, and risk the occasional clumsy word, you gradually begin to sense the meaning of what is being said. The confusing, overwhelming *sound* becomes more and more recognizable as speech, as full of meaning that you can understand. The third moment of theology begins when we start to sense that in and through all the noise and confusion, the grace and hope and grit and glory of the world, there is a deep conversation going on. It is a conversation between the Word of God and the One who speaks that Word. It is a conversation about the meaning of love, infinite love, and the words and phrases of the conversation are the very stuff of our universe—galaxies whirling into space, babies learning to crawl, enemies turning into friends. But even though our universe furnishes something of the eternal Son's conversation with the

Father, we are rarely capable of sensing that this is going on, let alone taking part in it.

If you know two old friends very well, you can usually sense some of the conversation that goes on without or beyond words—the winks or quizzical glances or well-used jokes. But how could any of us possibly sense the conversation going on in the rearing up of a mountain range or the birth of a child or the death of a butterfly? And yet, Christians believe, all these are part of the infinite conversation which is God's life. The Speaker speaks the eternal love and that love, being divine and infinitely living, takes form and sound and shape, is eternally the living Word of that living Speaker. And not content simply to enjoy this conversation between themselves, the Speaker and the Word, the Father and the Son, bring a universe into being as a term of endearment, a phrase in their eternal dialogue of love.

It is this conversation, so vast and awesome and beyond our imagination's grasp, that God desires to have us join. Indeed, we were created for that very purpose, created to be a pungent, peculiar, prickly but much-loved part of speech, created to participate in the communion which is God's very life. And in order to make it possible for us to hear the universe and ourselves in it as participants in God's conversation, God contracts the speaking into the framework of our world. God speaks the Word *into* our time and space as the historical human being Jesus. And as the Holy Spirit draws us *into* Jesus' life and fills us with his longing for the Father, we begin to sense this eternal conversation of love. We begin to learn this language by which Jesus and the Father converse, and to enter into their communion, their life. The One who draws us into their mutual giving life, the One who teaches us to cry out in their language, is God again—God the

Holy Spirit, who has from eternity been the love who draws the Speaker into speech, and fills the Word with yearning to speak the Speaker's Meaning, to do the will of the Father.

The first moment of theology is this divine speaking as it overtakes our lives, embracing all our stories and revealing them to be parts and pieces of God's story with us. The second moment of theology is when the loving power or Spirit of this Speaking inhabits us and transforms our hearts and minds so that we begin to hear and understand what God is saying, so that the Word takes root in us and unfolds to become the very pattern of our own lives. The third moment of theology is when, by the Spirit's power, we have been so drawn into the Word's human life and death and resurrection that we are able to hear the loving call of the Father as Jesus does and to cry out *"Abba"* in loving response, as he does. And from there, you could say, theology becomes *"theo-logia"* in its truest and deepest sense, God-talk: not in the sense of our talk about God, but rather God's talk, God's conversation and loving communion with God.

Now a word of warning. It scarcely needs to be said that this book will hardly be able to represent theology in either the second or the third moments. I cannot draw you into the mission of Christ, teach you to love with his heart and see with his eyes (the second moment). And I certainly cannot so imbue you with his relationship with the Father that you begin to join their conversation yourself (the third moment). But it is worth remembering that these are the reasons *why* we do theology. We do theology not to be clever or well-informed but in order to be drawn into God's own life.

Most of what we will be doing in this book will focus on the first moment of theology, the moment of recognizing the different ways God is speaking, the different mysteries by which God is present among us—creating, revealing, saving, re-creating. Nevertheless, I hope that we can explore these mysteries in such a way that we come to see them as invitations to meet and encounter God. Each mystery of faith is a different threshold, a different path into the one great and eternal mystery of God's life and our life in God.

∽ Theology as Prayer

Let me finish this chapter, then, by saying a little more about how theology can turn into prayer, or even how we can discover it as a form of prayer from the very beginning. Try this experiment to see something of the close kinship between theology and prayer. Think for a moment of someone you are presently not getting along with very well. How would you describe that person? Now take a few moments of silence and ask God to grant you a sense of the divine perspective on this same person, a sense perhaps of how Jesus is seeking to love this person, or even a sense of how God might desire to be present in your relationship with this person.

What did you discover? Many people find that, in ways they usually cannot explain, they begin to feel more open toward this other person. My own experience has often been that a deep well of patience and reconciliation is unstopped in me, filling me with the freedom to forgive and the strong humility to ask forgiveness. This deep wellspring, Christians believe, is the life of God itself—a pouring out of endless resource as God goes about the infinitely joyful work of being God, of being the Communion of Love, a work we see enacted in history as the story of Jesus. Theology, as it takes place in the eternity of God's own life, is this endless blissful communication of self-giving love; theology, as it takes place in the strain and struggle of our broken world, is the costly mission of Jesus to hear this self-giving love, to embody and enact this eternal communion, to *be* this reconciling Word of God. But it is this same *language* of communion that is theology—both in the bliss of heaven and the toil of earth—and it is this which opens our hearts toward one another, giving us eyes to see as God sees, a language in which to converse with one another right through the hurts we give.

In our world, the loving joy of the divine self-communication (theology) takes the form of being sent by the Father, being led by the Spirit, and giving ourselves freely in love into the hands of others—both divine and human. This was Jesus' daily struggle to "theologize," to interpret and make known the meaning of his relationship to the Father in their Spirit. If we come to live more theologically, then the rhythms and cadences of this language of divine self-communication will also become more natural, more native to our life. As we become more native speakers of theology, the language of God's life, we find ourselves able to communicate with reality ever more deeply, to sense something of that communion of love that the whole universe is created to enjoy. And it is the momentum of this divine communion, set loose in us through fellowship with Christ, that transforms our understanding, reconciling us to those we find difficult, breaking down walls of division, sending us into night shelters, turning us into chefs in soup kitchens. This is the embodied fruit of theology at work in us.

From this perspective, theology is the working out in disciplined reflection of what happens to us when we accept the call to take up our cross and follow Christ. I am saying, in other words (and this is the deepest premise of this book), that *theology and spiri-*

tuality are integrally related. In earlier eras of
Christianity this was the commonly held view: theology was seen as the attempt to understand and
explain what we as a community of prayer are
encountering in the course of our life together in
Christ. In one of the most famous formulations of
that period: "If you are a theologian, you pray in
truth; if you pray in truth, you are a theologian."[2]
God, we believe, draws us in various ways into the
divine communion, and this is what we call contemplation or prayer in its deepest sense: the gracious
drawing of our whole being into the divine heart.

Theology in our usual sense is the distillation into
human words and ideas of *the* Word who comes forth
from God and encounters us in prayer, drawing us
into the divine presence. But because of the distinction
between God's infinite holiness and the usual human
tendency to "know" things in a manipulative and con-
trolling way, we can only come to hear this divine
speech as we ourselves are liberated from sin and
transformed into the divine likeness—a process that
for us means nothing less than sharing in the paschal
mystery, the dying and rising of Christ.

The truth of God is not some *thing* we can "find
out" about God, it is simply the concrete form that
our encounter with God begins to take in our lives, in
works of love and words of faith, in ways of life and
habits of thought. Rowan Williams, one of
Anglicanism's wisest contemporary theologians,
writes:

> The end of the believer's life is knowledge of
> God in conformity to God. Knowledge of God is
> not a subject's conceptual grasp of an object, it
> is sharing what God is—more boldly, you might
> say, sharing God's "experience." God is known

in the exercise of crucifying compassion, if we
are like him in that, we know him.[3]

God is "speaking" our lives from the very heart of the
divine communion, and the very same Word who thus
calls us into being also calls us back again and again
into that communion. Christian theology is the
attempt to allow the divine meaning that rustles
through every page of our life story to be clarified and
highlighted by means of our fellowship with Christ
the Word made human flesh—and so finally to
become embodied in reflection and understanding.

So while we are exploring the mysteries of faith in
the chapters that follow, I hope you will be able to
sense each of these mysteries as an invitation to
prayer, a starting point for the journey into God's
conversation.

Chapter Two

The New Encounter with God

The Mystery of the Trinity

> For you did not receive a spirit of slavery to fall back into fear, but you have received a spirit of adoption. When we cry, "Abba! Father!" it is that very Spirit bearing witness with our spirit that we are children of God, and if children, then heirs, heirs of God and joint heirs with Christ— if, in fact, we suffer with him so that we may also be glorified with him.
>
> *Romans 8:15–17*

I was so cold I could barely stand still enough to see inside. The snow was falling in the moonlight and I remember how beautiful it was outside. But what I remember most was the sheer exuberant joy I felt at being allowed to stay up so late on Christmas Eve in order to share in what I could just barely see happening through the frosty windows of our home.

My family and I had just come back from the midnight service. My parents did not allow me to see any of my presents, even all wrapped up, until Christmas morning; I was the only one of four children who was still young enough to fall under this painful rule. But that night, for the first time, my parents said that while I could not join them and my siblings in bringing the presents from their hiding places to the foot of the Christmas tree, I could stay up and play outside in the new snow until they were finished.

What entranced me so on that snowy night long ago was not the glimpse of presents, although that was part of it. A deeper kind of marvel tantalized me as I watched my family moving through the house. It seemed that the happiness I could see on their faces and the bounty they carried in their arms were signs of all the love and joy I longed for in our life together. For a moment, though I stood outside peering in, I had been granted a vision of the secret heart and soul of our family. It was a procession of laughter and love that reminded me of the more solemn procession I had seen earlier that night during communion, people moving through a house with great gifts.

I have always loved the simple movement of life in a church. An empty room slowly fills as people trickle in, and soon it becomes a place of prayer filled with all the longing, hope, and pregnant quiet that prayer brings with it. Then a designated band moves up the aisle and into that mysterious space the altar gathers round itself. Later, another group with lights and sacred book comes back down into the people's midst, speaking a Word too intimate to be uttered from far away. Later still the whole place breaks into movement as the flow of communion draws all into its pattern of life poured out, given freely away.

In the last chapter I said that God communicates with us in mysteries. We are always being drawn across their thresholds into the infinite life within. And surely we are created longing to get in, to make a pilgrimage down the aisle toward Communion itself, to find the "lost lane end into heaven," to journey to the hidden heart of things. In perhaps his greatest short book, *The Weight of Glory*, C. S. Lewis shines a searching light on this longing of ours. It haunts us still, whether in the delighted laughter of our children or the image of another man giving his life for ours on a cross. Lewis suggests that this silent hunger we feel is a longing for *communion* with reality at its most intense. Far from merely wanting to *see* beautiful things, we want something impossible, hopeless, ridiculous: we want "to be united with the beauty we see, to pass into it, to receive it into ourselves, to bathe in it, to become part of it." The beauty and power we long to possess are only the whispers of One who cannot be possessed but who lives by giving all away freely in love. As Lewis writes,

> At present we are on the wrong side of the door. We discern the freshness and purity of the morning, but they do not make us fresh and pure. We cannot mingle with the splendours we see. But all the leaves of the New Testament are rustling with the rumour that it will not always be so. Some day, God willing, we shall get *in*.[1]

～ The First Disciples

Certainly the first followers of Jesus believed that in him the door had opened. Think of all those stories in scripture of great feasts and banquets and Jesus' apparent delight in them. In Jesus, an invitation to a great meal went out, and as his followers began to risk stepping over the threshold of the cross into the great communion on the other side, they were greeted not as unknown guests but as long-expected and well-beloved children. What exactly happened to those first followers of Jesus? We need to know the answer to this question, because their life with him changed the very way we encounter God.

The earliest Christians were convinced that God was at work in the world through the ministry of Jesus. They tried in various ways to describe the power and intimacy of God's presence in Jesus and certainly understood him to be God's anointed, the herald of a new dominion of God on earth. But what would this new dominion of God's justice look like, and how would it come? What would the role of Jesus and his disciples be?

Far from figuring out their theology from the very beginning, the early Christians found themselves overwhelmed by a presence, a Holy Spirit that led them back again and again to the pattern of their lives with Jesus. This pattern included their betrayal and fear as well as their healing and forgiveness. Some of his disciples may have wanted Jesus to become a pious memory, a precious "founder figure" whose image they would protect and tend. Instead, when they gathered together they found themselves being drawn back into their last meal with him, for he was alive with them in the breaking of the bread. Certain remembered words of his became like flame as they spoke them aloud: "Blessed are the poor in spirit, for theirs is the kingdom of heaven.... The time is fulfilled, and the kingdom of God has come near.... I am the bread of life, I am the good shepherd, I am the true vine and you are the branches."

Gradually his disciples realized that fellowship with Jesus was not something they would master once and for all. Instead, Jesus knit them together in a new way as the risen Christ became the very pattern of their life. As St. Paul soon realized, believers were becoming the new Body of Christ, a new creation, and in this fellowship with him and one another they were coming to know someone else—someone whom Jesus himself always turned to, someone he taught them to address in prayer as "our Father in heaven."

The early Christians had not been given a new idea about God—they were still faithful Jews. Rather, it was as if the Spirit that had been sent to them was plunging them not only into Christ's life, but into his own relationship with the One he called *Abba*. They began to cry out to him not in a spirit of fear, but with Christ's own Spirit, seeking to know the Father as Jesus knows him—and to know *themselves* as God's beloved, God's lost and returning prodigals, God's children.

We have three kinds of evidence that tell us this is what happened: the witness of the scriptures, the earliest patterns of eucharistic worship, and the common life of the church. Each testifies to the divine momentum that was shaping the early community into the Body of Christ. What these early followers discovered was a new way of encountering God through the mystery of God's own life on earth. That is, they understood with increasing clarity that Jesus' own life was simply and purely a relationship with the One he called Father and whom they knew as the God of Israel. And it was into this relationship between Jesus and the Father that the early Christians were brought.

The shape of the new community, furthermore, was based on this new encounter. In baptism, the power of the Spirit brought creation out of chaos and led the community into the death and resurrection of Jesus. In the eucharist, it was the same Spirit who drew Mary's faithfulness into the purposes of God that now received them and their offerings as the living presence of God's Word. Thus Jesus' early followers began to grow into a new identity, one shaped less by their families and backgrounds and more by the relationships they developed with each other through a common fidelity to Christ. That is why St. Paul could write: "As many of you as were baptized into Christ have clothed yourselves with Christ. There is no longer Jew or Greek, there is no longer slave or free, there is no longer male and female; for all of you are one in Christ Jesus" (Galatians 3:27-28). In all this they learned to live into what made Jesus who he was: his relationship to the Father in the Spirit. In this sense, every follower acquired a new identity, one achieved through communion and expressed and lived out in baptism and eucharist.

Two points are crucial here. First, the early community provided new ways for its followers to relate to each other and to God; and second, what gave life and shape to that new way of relationship was none other than God's own self-giving way of life. Jesus' followers, in other words, were invited into the mystery of God's own way of being God. They were invited to risk living into that pattern of death and resurrection that marks the earthly form of God's life.

So the joy I felt as a child in glimpsing my family through the window on Christmas Eve was indeed a sign of all our longing to gaze upon the love at the heart of things. The patterns and movement of our common life are sacraments of something greater and deeper: that pattern of eternal loving, giving, and receiving that is the only fruitful ground of all our relationships. Our yearning for communion with beauty in all its many forms whispers to us of the Holy Spirit, who would draw us into Communion itself: the communion of Father, Son, and Holy Spirit that is God's own life.

～ God's Trinitarian Life

The early Christians' sense of being forgiven and freed, of being *re-created* in Christ, was the formative influence in their common life. It led them to see that both Jesus and the Spirit who had drawn them into Jesus' life must be related to the Father in some extraordinarily intimate way. After all, it was God the Father who claimed them as newly reborn children. But it was also God who lived among them through the life, death, and resurrection of the Son, and who spoke the Word that called them from their old lives into a new creation. And, once again, it was God working within them as Spirit who fashioned in them the mind of God's beloved Son and allowed them to share in Christ's fellowship with the Father. This same God accepted them into eternal love, embodied that love among them, and poured that love into their hearts through the knowledge of Christ.

As the early Christians looked back upon the history of Israel they could see this threefold pattern embedded in the whole story. In the beginning, the divine breath "swept over the face of the waters" and prepared the cosmos to receive the divine creative Word: "Then God said, 'Let there be light'; and there was light" (Genesis 1:2-3). In the beginning of the new creation, Mary of Nazareth is told: "The Holy Spirit will come upon you, and the power of the Most High will overshadow you" (Luke 1:35). Mary's faithfulness is drawn by the Spirit into the purposes of God, thus bringing to birth in her a human response to the divine speaking, the incarnation of the Word. For St. Paul, the Spirit was the power of God bringing forth the next stage of this new creation by raising Jesus from the dead (Romans 1:4). In the resurrection, the Spirit presents the living and crucified Word to the community of the church, thus continuing to bring forth from the old creation a new response to the Word. The birth pangs of the new creation continue, as the community born at Pentecost still struggles today to embody and give voice to the Word.

How did the early Christians begin to make sense of the Trinity? They saw that this new encounter with God was not the same as meeting God in three different roles or activities, just as I can be the celebrant at the eucharist, the coffee hour host, and an exasperated parent all on the same Sunday morning. For them the Trinity was not a divine game of peek-a-boo in which a playful deity peeps out at them from behind different masks (now the ancient fellow with the beard, now the infant, now the bird, and so on) until God tires of the whole charade. No, when these Christians met God they were swept up into God's own *inner life* of mutual relationships. The Word who becomes incarnate and the Spirit who moves over the chaos of human hearts are not *temporary* patch-up efforts on the part of a bumbling deity who had not quite counted on human recalcitrance. Instead, Word and Spirit are *eternally* enacting the communion who is God, and into this communion Christians are drawn. For the Father is never just Father, but eternally delights to pour himself out, give himself away in the "othering," the speaking, of the Word. The delight that draws the Father beyond simple oneness toward Another is the same love, the same Spirit, who likewise draws forth from the Word an eternal response of loving self-surrender to the Father.

God is love. In that powerful statement, Christians have come to understand that God is God through relationship: the communion of Lover, Beloved, and Enrapturer. Just as Christians grow into the fullness of who they truly are through their lives together, the *relationality* of God is precisely who God is. In other words, it is through the eternal loving and self-giving of one to another that the Persons of God are Persons. The Father pours out the divine life to the Son, the Son speaks and embodies this life, and the Spirit brings both together in passionate delight and love.

So what does it mean to say that Christians are living into the communion of three Persons? Do you ever have those moments when you sense that you are not really "being yourself"? Certain situations seem to change us into bright, brittle caricatures of ourselves, such as meeting a future mother-in-law for the first time, going out to lunch with a boss, speaking at the annual golf dinner of the local association of morticians. I have always found that such times evoke a dizzy stiltedness in my sense of self. And if they are prolonged—if we work for years alongside colleagues who swap ethnic jokes all day for light relief—before we know it, we are chameleon souls forever trying to blend into the prevailing muzak.

By contrast, to be led by the Spirit into Christian fellowship is liberating and life-giving, and that is really our starting point. St. Paul's letters are filled with instructions for life together in the community, not just because Paul was a trifle bossy but because he had a vision of what a community trying to live out the life of Christ would look like. Above all, it would be a place where the slow and sometimes painful struggle to love one another would draw us out of those cramped caricatures we *think* of as ourselves and into a new pattern of life, a new *identity*. For Paul, our new personhood is one of relationship: as Christians we become persons whose sense of self emerges out of our common journey with others, our life of mutual giving and receiving. So the Christian life is a journey from baptism into our new identity toward a deeper discovery of who we really are by means of our relationships with God and one another, celebrated in the eucharist. We are able to celebrate this new relational identity in the eucharist precisely because it is the event in which we come to be with one another by sharing in Jesus' being with the Father, in his thanksgiving, in his eucharist.

In much the same way, we have all experienced times when a new set of friends or a new job seem to bring out the best in us. I will never forget the sense of liberation I felt my first year in college: suddenly I was surrounded by new friends who did not think my tastes in music were weird, who liked poetry and political debating even more than I did, and who made me feel welcome as myself in their midst. I was beginning to discover who I had it in me to become: I felt I was being invited to *be a person* for the first time in my life. Similarly, but in a far deeper way, the early Christians discovered that their truest and strongest sense of self grew out of their new relationships with one another, which were the means by which God was inviting them into divine relationship.

In John's gospel we see Jesus teaching the disciples about the essential connection between the Father's love for him as Son and their need to let this same love be at work in them:

> As the Father has loved me, so I have loved you; abide in my love. If you keep my commandments, you will abide in my love, just as I have kept my Father's commandments and abide in his love. . . . This is my commandment, that you love one another as I have loved you. No one has greater love than this, to lay down one's life for one's friends. You are my friends if you do what I command you. I do not call you servants any longer, because the servant does not know

> what the master is doing; but I have called you
> friends, because I have made known to you
> everything that I have heard from my Father.
> (John 15:9-15)

The logic of this passage is remarkable. John understands Jesus to be making the disciples into his friends
by showing them his own relationship with the
Father. His relation to the Father is one of being infinitely loved and of loving infinitely in return. What is
so interesting for our purposes is that this loving,
when it is acted out in our world, takes a particular
form: namely, the communal love of the disciples for
each other that finds its ultimate form in the love
which lays down even life itself for one's friends. The
Spirit groans in bringing to birth the infinite mutual
love of the divine Persons within the Christian community, and the only adequate sign this infinite love
can find—on the horizontal plane of history—is the
willingness of love to give up life for another.

Obviously, Christians did not constantly jump off
cliffs to impress each other with their mutual love.
Nevertheless, what Jesus had done for them and, in a
sense, *to* them by making them his friends and loving
them even at the cost of his life—this remains an abiding "commandment." This willingness to be created as
one's true self by being *for the other* becomes the deep
law of the Christian communal life, investing even a
cup of cold water offered to one in need with the vast
significance of sacrificial love. What I am suggesting is
that there is a crucial, indeed a divine connection
between being a real person and being freely available
for the call of sacrificial love.

∽ Becoming a Person

Throughout this chapter I use the word "person" quite a bit, which is a very ambiguous word. On the one hand, it might mean a self-contained, self-sufficient ego with no need of anybody else; on the other, it can mean someone whose identity is tied up with relationships. I have been arguing that we are persons *through* our friends or spouse or children. Becoming a person means loving and caring for others: we all know that we would not have developed into persons without innumerable others smiling us into smiling back and talking us into talking. It is how we are drawn into the world of fellowship with others.

The gospel vision of Jesus shows us a wonderfully vibrant and powerful person who understands that his very existence is to do his Father's will, to be in relationship with the Father. He is led by the Spirit to fulfill his identity by speaking and acting out the Father's love: "The Spirit of the Lord is upon me, because he has anointed me to bring good news to the poor" (Luke 4:18). Thus Jesus' life was one of wonder and trust as he searched his heart, listening for the Spirit to lead him into the truth of who he was called to be.

That is our vocation, too, as we seek to become "persons." As we let the Holy Spirit guide us into Jesus' own hunger to know the Father's will, so we begin to echo that yearning and embark on our own search for the direction of our lives. The freedom and love with which Jesus hands himself over to the Father liberates us in turn from all the fears and idols that obscure the Spirit's invitation to be real persons. The Spirit of God fills us with Jesus' freedom in the One he calls Father, and in him we begin to discover the bravest, gladdest possibilities of our own person-hood. We are called out of ourselves, away from self-preoccupation and into the real needs and situations of others.

But in our world, to act in love is more difficult than it first appears. The life of love has been bitterly interrupted and broken down; the cross teaches us that loving too much will put our life at risk. In such a world, becoming a person seems more like agony than bliss or peace. Things are turned upside down: self-giving seems more like sacrifice, more the undoing of true personhood than its fulfillment. That is why the saving power of Christ lies in his willingness to accept this risk. Jesus struggles to be fully a person *within* the broken fragments of human existence. That is why the pattern by which Jesus lives out his identity—the pattern of his relationship with the Father—leads him to his death. Jesus' prayer takes the form of the sacrifice of the cross, and the Father's answer in the Spirit is the resurrection. Herbert McCabe puts it incisively:

> He is not first of all an individual person who then prays to the Father, his prayer to the Father is what constitutes him as who he is. He is not just one who prays, not even one who prays best, he is sheer prayer. In other words the crucifixion/resurrection of Jesus is simply the showing forth, the visibility in human terms, in human history, of the relationship to the Father which constitutes the person who is Jesus. The prayer of Jesus which is his crucifixion, his absolute renunciation of himself in love to the Father, is the eternal relationship of Father and Son made available as part of our history, part of the web of mankind of which we are fragments, a part of the web that gives it a new centre, a new pattern.[2]

This is the miracle of God's grace. that the whole creation is included within the embrace of Father, Son, and Holy Spirit.

God has chosen not to be God without us. We have been invited not merely to "have a relationship" with God but, far more intimately, to become participants ourselves in the divine relationship, the Trinity. The whole cosmos comes into being *within* the mutual loving of the divine Persons, so that neither the glory nor the trauma of our world is remote from God. But creation is not a magic show that God orders up as a form of celestial entertainment. No, all the mysteries of our faith—creation, revelation, incarnation, redemption, the church, the coming dominion of God's love—are the language in which God the Holy Trinity speaks its infinite love and fruitfulness into time and space. That loving self-giving stretches across entire universes to give life, and across the far greater divide between holiness and sin.

Philosopher Simone Weil speaks movingly of this costly "stretching apart" of the Trinity to embrace a universe of time:

> God did not create anything except love itself, and the means to love. He created love in all its forms. He created beings capable of love from all possible distances. Because no other could do it, he himself went the greatest possible distance, the infinite distance. This distance between God and God, this supreme tearing apart, this agony beyond all others, this marvel of love, is the crucifixion. Nothing can be further from God than that which has been made accursed. This tearing apart, over which supreme love places the bond of supreme union, echoes perpetually across the universe in the midst of silence, like

two notes, separate yet melting into one, like pure and heart-rending harmony. This is the Word of God. The whole creation is nothing but its vibration. When human music in its greatest purity pierces our soul, this is what we hear through it. When we have learned to hear the silence, this is what we grasp more distinctly through it.[3]

Simone Weil had struggled through her own chronic illness to share the suffering of the French during World War II. She knew personally how a life of terrible affliction can make people feel lost and separated from hope and from God. But through her own spiritual journey into the heart of the gospel, Weil began to sense that there was a greater, even infinite "separation" within the very life of God. By analogy we might think of the relationship of life-long friends. It is not closed and exclusive but shows its true depths as it opens up to include others. The stronger the relationship, the more it is able to extend, to stretch apart to embrace all kinds of new friends and hopes and fears. Or think of the relationship of a wife and husband, embracing within their love the suffering of a child: the pain and hurt of the child actually comes into and is healed within the loving relationship of the parents as they stretch out their relationship to include the child.

Simone Weil believed that what we see happening in Christ on the cross is the stretching out of God to us in our affliction and separation from hope. There, in Jesus' cry of dereliction, we see the Word of God finding us, sharing our plight, crying out to the Father. Our lostness and distance from each other and from God has been embraced within the "distance" of God's eternal life of love, embraced within the love of the Father for the Son and the love of the Son for the Father, that one love—the bond of supreme union, as Simone Weil puts it—whom we know as God the Holy Spirit. The whole creation echoes with this loving of the divine Persons, a loving which in heaven is pure joy but which in our broken world sounds like a "heart-rending harmony," a child crying, a victim suffering. But within and beyond all suffering of every kind is the infinite mutual self-giving of the divine Persons. And our suffering is forever embraced and suffered within this eternal loving which is God's life. This mystery of the Trinity is the deepest response Christianity can make to the problems of suffering and evil in our world.

∽ The Unity of God
The previous section explored briefly the threefold character of God. But what does God's "threeness" imply for our worship? How can we speak of God as "one God, the maker of heaven and earth," as we do every Sunday in church in the creeds and in so many of our prayers? How can we talk about God as Trinity without becoming "tri-theists," with the Father, the Son, and the Holy Spirit seen as three separate and individual gods, or without simply submerging the three Persons of the Trinity into one bland, undifferentiated mass? We need a way of talking about God's unity so that we can make sense of the Christian way of talking about God as One in three Persons.

The early church was no stranger to these questions. For some early Christians, one way of safeguarding the unity of God was to say that the Persons of the Trinity were simply temporary; each mode of being was a temporary way that God related to us at different points in our history. But the church came to reject this view, which was incompatible with its experience of being called into existence as a community of love dwelling within an infinite communion of eternally loving Persons. Similarly, the early church rejected attempts to claim that Son and Spirit are subordinate deities who are somehow lesser than the Father, for the community knew that in God there is "one equal music," as John Donne put it, in which the Father never somehow "holds back" anything from the Son or Spirit. Furthermore, as Roman Catholic theologian Elizabeth Johnson has rightly warned, in this view there is a danger of stressing a notion of self-giving love in God that ends up reinforcing models of subordination and oppression. She argues that trinitarian theology can and must conceive of the Trinity in ways that highlight *mutuality* rather than *subordination*. From this perspective the oneness of God is discovered precisely in the free *act* of love by which the three Persons of the Trinity choose to give all to each other.[4]

Part of the confusion comes from our peculiar notions of the self, which stress individuality rather than interdependence. We assume that "person" means a solitary "I" peering out gingerly at the world rather than a conversation in which I become more and more myself by means of my fellowship with others. So we have to ask carefully what we mean by terms such as "personhood" and "unity." As the Anglican theologian Leonard Hodgson has pointed out, we can distinguish between *mathematical* unity and *organic* unity. "We arrive at the mathematical type of unity," says Hodgson, "by eliminating all multiplicity."[5] While this is fine for numbers, creatures seem to have a more richly complex unity. In fact, the more "advanced" the living being, the more complex its unity. The amoeba is about as close to mathematical unity as living things can get, but that is not much of a recommendation.

So perhaps we can look at the oneness of God by taking an analogy not from what we know of numbers, but from human beings. Our unity is more complicated. It not only embraces the biological variety of our own bodies, but extends to include the whole psychological and spiritual network of relationships that are part of being a human person. I am who I am through the persons who love and have loved me, and through the personal disciplines I exercise—sometimes painful, sometimes delightful—in going beyond myself to love others. It is true that, psychologically speaking, we can feel that our unity and stability as persons is threatened and even overwhelmed by our efforts to sustain the integrity of all our relationships, past and present. On the other hand, we count it as a strength and sign of great personal integrity when we are able to go through life without splitting off aspects of ourselves by rejecting relationships that are difficult to integrate and accept.

Although a great deal of classical Christian thinking about God's unity was influenced by the ancient Greek ideal of mathematical unity, our more recent awareness of another kind of unity—an organic, richly complex unity built on relationships—may be more helpful here. If we are trying to find an analogy for divine unity, Hodgson writes, "We obviously think more truly if we try to move upwards beyond human personality to a richer organic unity, than if we descend through amoebae and atoms in an attempt to reach a pure mathematical unity." Although *mathematical* unity is marked by decreasing multiplicity, *organic* unity is complex:

> The greater the complexity of the organism, the
> more intense must be the unifying power of the

life which pervades and unifies.... The most intense unity of which we have experience on earth is that which is required to unify a human personality; if we believe that God is a unity unifying three distinct Persons, our faith implies that the unity of God is a more intense unity, a higher degree of unity, than any unity known to us in creation.[6]

And, I would hasten to add, it is a unity *achieved* through the embrace of complexity, *constituted* by the infinite self-sharing of Father, Son, and Spirit, and *accomplished* through the events of the gospel narratives. We do not really know the strength of this divine unity apart from the resurrection of Jesus from the dead. Although the Son entered the deepest corners of human alienation from God, the resurrection reveals that the unity of God is not exhausted but glorified. For within the unity of divine loving, God has embraced not only what is *other* than God (the creature) but even that which is *antagonistic* to God (the sinner).

Of course, this victory of the divine unity works itself out during the passing of time. In a sense God has chosen freely to accept the risk of time. The life, death, resurrection, and ascension of Jesus, and the sending of the Spirit upon the church, all demonstrate the unity of divine love. For God these events are not "over with," as though they were just unfortunate episodes that God has managed to get past, but remain spiritual realities. We are always being drawn to participate in them anew, at deeper and deeper levels of our own journeys as Christians, both individually through prayer and meditation and corporately through the eucharist.

So we could say that there is in God's own eternal communion a self-sharing that is infinitely beyond history and that is already infinite. St. Paul wrote of the self-emptying of Jesus in taking the form of a servant (Philippians 2:7) and perhaps this eternal self-emptying of one Person for another is the basis for the events we see taking place historically. All the acts of love and self-surrender God undertakes in time are the merest whisper of the self-giving that goes on forever among the Persons of the Trinity. All the humiliations of Jesus, even his sense of separation from the Father, are finite expressions in the broken language of time of the eternal and loving self-outpouring that constitutes God's life.

Does this mean that what happens to Jesus and to us does not, somehow, *matter* to God? One classical Christian response has been to say *no*, God is not dependent on the universe; our existence does not matter at all to God, even if we ceased this very moment to exist. Another response goes to the opposite extreme and insists that our history is the very means by which God is becoming fully God. But this would mean that God could not exist without us creatures, a way of thinking that most Christians through the centuries have rejected.

I would prefer to say that if we stick close to the church's sense of being drawn into the communion of the Trinity, then our history *does* matter to God. God is not dependent on what happens in history or even on there being any history at all to happen. But what does matter to God is that every estrangement that is overcome becomes a *flowering* of one of the infinite possibilities of loving and unity found in God. What matters is that every lost soul who is found, every hurt child who is healed, every sinner who turns from wickedness and lives is the fruit of the divine unity.

We could say that each of these events is the gift of the divine Persons, one to another. The mending of our brokenness is cause for rejoicing in heaven, because it is all part of the delighted activity of mutual loving that is the Trinity.

Imagine a wife and husband who have a flower garden. They enjoy it very much. But when one of them makes a bouquet and brings it to the other as a token of love, then the flowers matter to each of them in a new and profound way. They not only exist, pleasantly enough, as flowers to be gazed at, but they have also been drawn in and made part of that language by which the lovers commune with each other. The particular color and scent of these flowers also matters: it is the detail in which this love has been expressed. Even the story of each flower matters: this one came through the painful episode of the rose-eating deer, that one blew over in a storm but was splinted and bloomed again. Before, when the flowers were just there, these things were interesting but they did not really signify much. Now that they have been taken up into a gift from one spouse to another, they are invested with a treasurable weight, for they in themselves have become also the words of a *conversation* and the means of love.

Similarly, in the loving self-sharing of the Trinity there exist—like flowers in this garden—infinite possibilities of divine love. But when in acts of creation and re-creation these possibilities come alive, then we and our history matter to God in a new way. For that is how we are taken up to share in the divine communion, not only as possibilities but also as creatures, as reconciled children, through whom the persons of the Trinity have chosen to give themselves in love, one to another. We matter to God not because God depends on us in order to be God, but because in and through the activity of creating, redeeming, and sanctifying us God has freely chosen a communion of love and freedom. Each event of God's work in our lives—and our response—becomes an act of self-sharing, a way of loving. It is like the bouquet whose flowers become meaningful in a new way as the language by which lovers commune with each other.

So you can imagine yourself as a cherished partner in the conversation that is God's life. God the Holy Spirit may inspire you, for example, to love some difficult person as Jesus would—thus you are drawn into the conversation between Jesus and the Spirit. In Jesus, and through your share in his ministry, you yourself become more and more a part of Christ's loving exchange with the Father—discerning his will more clearly in your life, receiving ever more fully his love for you as the very constitution of your identity, your personhood. You are becoming who you are precisely because in you the Father is loving the Beloved, and that same Beloved—Christ-in-you—is returning the Father's love with all the joy and power of the Holy Spirit.

～ Doctrine at Work: Why Pray?

We could say that this mystery of God's communal life is the lens by which we come to a deeper understanding of everything. For if the eternal self-sharing of the Trinity is the ground of everything that is, then in some way there must be a beauty and a hidden logic that we will come to understand more fully as we enter into its heart. The question is whether we can learn how to apply the wisdom of trinitarian living to our everyday life.

So let us take a practice case and see if the doctrine of the Holy Trinity can be put to work. Consider the question of prayer. Why do we pray? God already knows everything, so isn't it presumptuous to think we could somehow "get" God to do something? Is prayer just between us and God, with us as pitiful creatures abject before the Almighty, hoping to wring some little concession from the divine mercy? Certainly we have more than a few clues that this is a false picture indeed. Jesus taught the disciples that the first words to say in prayer are "Our Father," so our prayer must be something we do in fellowship with Jesus, namely, talking with his Father and ours. In turn, that means we are talking not to an anonymous and inscrutable deity but to someone Jesus knows intimately and whom we are being invited to know in him. We have Paul's numerous references to the role of the Holy Spirit in our prayer, particularly in his letter to the Romans: "For we do not know how to pray as we ought, but that very Spirit intercedes with sighs too deep for words" (Romans 8:26). Paul suggests that we better give up the idea that we are the ones praying at all: it is the Spirit who prays in us, moving us deeply and uniting our heart with the heart of God. How does the Holy Spirit do this? By filling our hearts with the heart of Christ. By allowing Christ's prayer, his conversation, with the Father to come to life as the very center of our own life: "When we cry, 'Abba! Father!' it is that very Spirit bearing witness with our spirit that we are children of God . . . and joint heirs with Christ" (Romans 8:15-17).

If God is God because of the loving communion of the Trinity, then when we pray we are invited more deeply into this exchange of love. Prayer is really God happening in us, you could say, or—more accurately— our coming into fuller being as we pray in the divine communion. So when we ask for things in prayer, we are not trying to coax God into doing something God had never thought of until we happened along with

the bright idea. Instead, God is trying to renew our
minds and hearts in the likeness of the divine yearning. For what is it that we want, really? Admit it. We
want an ice cream cone or a bowl of popcorn, a nicer
house or a shorter commute to work. That does not
sound much like the yearning of the Son for the
Father, you say. All right, but it is a starting place!
Imagine if you did not desire, did not love, did not
hunger for anything at all. Prayer is all about letting
the loving of the divine Persons deepen in us and
stretch our small, feeble desires into a deeper desire,
one that sets us free to be truly ourselves, truly
persons in communion.

> If we are honest enough to admit to our shabby
> infantile desires, then the grace of God will grow
> in us, it will slowly be revealed to us, precisely
> in the course of our prayer, that there are more
> important things that we do truly want. But
> this will not be some abstract recognition that
> we ought to want these things, we will really
> discover a desire for them in ourselves. But we
> must start from where we are.[7]

The point is that prayer is not about us sitting outside
the heavenly gates, for we have already been let into
the heart of heaven. The work of prayer is the activity
of God the Holy Spirit freeing us from the grasping,
frightened, self-important bundles of instincts we have
been taught to *think* of as our true selves in order
to discover the deep, strong, and passionate person
we are created to become in Christ. As we are drawn
into his stance before the Father, we are given the freedom and clarity of vision to want truly and desire
authentically.

Do you see how this works? The idea is to set the
question or issue that arises within a new framework.

The aim is to let the most appropriate doctrines permeate your thinking about something in a way that reconfigures the issues and casts them in a deeper light. You could take the problem of never having enough volunteers to run the soup kitchen or how to improve inadequate programs for kids trying to avoid gangs, or the question of whether your congregation should begin celebrating a Spanish-language liturgy, or whatever the Spirit is calling you to mindfulness about. With practice you will learn to sense which doctrines will be most pertinent and how to unpack the issues involved in terms of the logic of the doctrines at hand. Chances are, the doctrine of the Trinity will be deeply illuminating no matter what question you need to address, but now it is time to consider some others.

Chapter Three

The Splendor of God

The Mystery of Creation

> For it is the God who said, "Let light shine out
> of darkness," who has shone in our hearts to
> give the light of the knowledge of the glory of
> God in the face of Jesus Christ.
>
> *2 Corinthians 4:6*

What would you think if I told you that Christians believe God does not exist? And yet it is true that in a universe where we believe that golf balls and my dog and Rembrandt and subatomic particles all *exist*—in such a universe God does *not* exist. God is not one of those items in the universe. Rather, God is the answer to the question, why does anything exist at all? God, Christians believe, is the one who causes everything that exists to exist. Notice what this means about God.

Suppose I came along and said to you that I had a special scientific instrument and, for a nominal fee, I would be delighted to let you look into it so you would be able to see God. Why, besides a healthy suspicion of such offers, might you have the feeling you would not get your money's worth? "Because," you would say to me, "if God is just some object out there, then who made God?"

Once we are talking about an existing thing, no matter how wondrous or invisible or powerful, then the question can always arise: how did this thing come to be? By "God," Jews and Christians and Muslims all mean the One who is not among all the beings that are but is rather the giver of all being, the author of all life, the maker of heaven and earth. And that means that God cannot be one of those things that has existence, for then we could ask, who gave God existence? God did not get the job of being God because God is somehow bigger, tougher, and smarter than the rest of us. God is not the highest and mightiest of all existing beings, but the source of all beings.

Or as the thirteenth-century theologian Thomas Aquinas liked to say, God is the sheer act of existence itself. The things we are used to—stars, eyelashes, pickle relish, and so on—all exist as particular things. Let's take pickle relish. Its essence is to be, well, really good pickle relish. But while the essence of pickle relish is to be sweet and sour, tart and crunchy, it is *not* of the essence of pickle relish that it must *exist*. In other words, for pickle relish, as for all creatures, to be *something* and simply *to be* are quite distinct matters. Though it pains me to admit it, it is quite possible that there might not be any actual pickle relish in existence. It is not part of the definition of pickle relish that it must exist. And that is a crucial difference between the Creator and all creatures. For while essence and existence are two quite different things for creatures, the very essence of God is to exist—not as *something*, but as the sheer loving act of existing itself. As you may have noticed, however, this means that existence is *not* part of the definition of a creature. Every creature that actually exists is a startling, won-

drous, and utterly surprising event of God's giving
life. Which is why we call God the Creator, the giver
of existence.

Christians have usually tried to state this truth as
the doctrine of "creation out of nothing." The doctrine
functions like a grammatical principle: whenever you
talk about the world and God, make sure that whatever you say points to the universe being entirely the
free gift of God and God alone. It means that God does
not just shuffle around a bunch of eternally existing
bits and pieces of potential universes. God does something more miraculous. In love and freedom, God
chooses to call into existence that which has no existence. God pours out the power of existence itself so
that everything which comes to be will have a share
in this power of existence, will share according to its
kind in the activity of existing. In a way, this is the
most miraculous feature of the Christian doctrine of
creation: God does not just pretend to make a dragonfly—making a little body, and wings that God has to
move really fast to make it zip around the way drag-
onflies are supposed to do. No, God creates a dragonfly by giving it the power to be itself, which is a share
in God's own power to be, to exist. In the same way,
God is creating *you* this very moment. You are really
there, a miraculous, freely loved-into-existence being.
And God is doing that in your case by giving you the
power to be *yourself.* Neither you nor I nor anything
else need ever have existed; we *exist* because God
delights and chooses that we should. Existence is
God's free gift.

∾ **Creation as the Activity of Trinitarian Love**
After reading the last chapter on the Trinity, you may
be wondering (or at least I hope you are!) how God's
creative activity fits in with the mystery of God's *trini-*

tarian life. If we understand God as the source of all existence, who freely wills to give life to Another (the Son), then we are beginning to recognize that the very same love which marks God's life as trinitarian communion is also the intimate and continual source of the universe's existing. God is God because the Father freely wills to pour out existence to the Son—who *is* Son by lovingly entrusting this giving-life, Holy Spirit, back to the Father: "Father, into your hands I commend my Spirit" (Luke 23:46). We learn about this infinite bestowal of love in the story of Jesus and come to share in it through our life of common prayer. And it is precisely this trinitarian life that is the glorious reason why there is a universe at all rather than simply nothing.

So what does this mean? It means that we and all things come into being as a free act of that very same love. Everything that exists is part of the Son's wonderful declaration of the Father's love. The Son chooses to express this infinite, giving life as an infinite return of love to the Father. And the same Love who draws Father and Son into communion also draws them to include the creation of the universe as the very language of this divine communion. One analogy to this trinitarian activity of creation is the coming into being of a family. The love of two persons for one another draws them into ever deeper communion, and this loving communion becomes expressed and embodied in the gift of children. Soon there is a whole new world coming into being: diapers, middle-of-the-night feedings, unbelievable amounts of laundry, and, before you know it, extremely inexperienced drivers wanting to borrow the car. And yet for all the exhaustion, frustration, and occasional heartbreak, each element of this new family world has within it the secret signs of the love that begets and nourishes it.

Parents learn how to speak their love for each other even through the purchase of a nifty new diaper pail as well as through the smiles they give each other on their children's faces. The Son speaks his love for the Father by bringing ever more concrete possibilities of existence into being: every galaxy, every mountain range, every act of compassion among men and women—these are all the very alphabet of the Word's speaking of the Father's infinite love. The sheer existence of anything at all speaks to us of the infinite self-sharing that identifies the Father. But more than that, the pattern, the order, the *logos* by which everything comes to be precisely and truly its own unique self speaks to us—is the speaking to us—of the Father's Word, that divine *Logos* whom we know, John's gospel tells us, as the Word made flesh, Jesus of Nazareth.

Just as God does not exist as God by a bare inchoate being but rather by a pattern of relationship, of loving communion, so too the Father's Word does not speak of the divine love just by giving us bare existence but by imbuing all reality with the whispers and glimmers of that infinite structure of relationship, of patterns of loving, by which God's life takes place. And it is this infinite pattern and meaning, or *Logos*, that is at play in all the ordered laws and patterns by which every creature comes to be and is itself. Just as two parents each have their particular "signature," those unmistakable character traits that peek out in the particular look of a child's eyes or imbue their home with a certain feeling, so too the whole universe echoes with the signature of the Father's endless self-giving and the Son's loving speaking of the Father's giving and the powerful tide of the Spirit's beckoning.

Rarely do we see this so clearly as in that aspect of creation which bears the divine image: humanity. For here we can see writ small the rhythm of divine life—something hard to make out exactly in the vast expanse of interstellar space. What is this divine rhythm implicit in the ebb and flow of the creation? All reality, gift as it is of the trinitarian communion, is most fulfilled as *what it is* by moving freely toward love and fellowship. This is what, apart from sin, we might be able to see in the particular freedom and love by which human beings give themselves to each other. By contrast, as long as I try to exist by viewing the rest of the world either as a competitor or as an object to be possessed, I remain isolated and (in varying degrees of nastiness) more or less sub-human. I become most fully alive, most securely and wondrously who I have it in me to be, not by guarding myself from the taint of others' lives, but by freely entering into loving communion with them. Unfortunately, we human beings have managed to organize things so that this vulnerable and loving availability of one to another can only be accomplished through much pain and at the risk of self-sacrifice. What ought to have been a free and delighted presence to one another—in the created image of God's trinitarian life—becomes laden with deep misunderstandings and the bitterness begotten of historic wrongs. Our lives are so painfully fragile and pressed for survival that even the religious call to self-giving inevitably becomes only one more oppression.

∽ Hearing God's Meaning in the Universe

I have suggested that God creates the whole universe as an expression of the loving relationships of the Trinity. This ought to mean that we could "overhear" something of God's inner life in the life of creation.

Suppose, for example, that you and your best friend have taken a bike trip together each year for as long as you can remember. One year, at the end of the trip, your friend gives you a little box. At first it seems like just a strange collection of pebbles and dried flowers and sea shells; in fact it *is* a strange collection of these things. But the more you look at them, the more they begin to speak to you in marvelously evocative ways of all your bike trips. There is one item from each trip you have made over the years, each item lovingly selected and preserved by your friend for you, and the meaning that comes through the whole collection is nothing less than your years of friendship together.

The universe is a collection like this, a strange but poignantly moving assemblage of gifts, and the meaning of the whole is nothing less than the eternal outpouring of love that is God's trinitarian life. Each and every creature is a gift of the Father to the Son and the Son to the Father in their Spirit. So what do we overhear when we listen to the universe as a divine gift? There is the miraculous fact that each thing which exists *does* exist, and that this happens out of nothing except the freely loving self-sharing of God's life; this is a sign for us of the eternal, free decision of the Father to pour out the divine life as Son and Spirit. There are all the patterns and harmonies and laws of nature enabling everything that exists to become the particular and cherishable being that it is; and these ordered structures are the echoes in time and space of the eternal Word speaking forth the patterned relationships of God's communion. And there is the energy by which every creature is drawn to live into the *fullness* of its being—not just to exist as a lion or a lamb, but to be fully and completely a lion and a lamb precisely by being the particular lion or lamb they have it in them to be. And this momentum pulling everything toward its goal is the same yearning desire or Holy Spirit by which the Father and the Son are who they are by giving themselves away to each other.

The most fundamental aspects of creation, therefore, reflect in a stunning and miraculous way the abiding, eternal relationships of the divine Persons to one another. A rose, for all its beauty, speaks to us of a beauty beyond imagining. It is always the sign to us of the Father's free giving, the Son's eternal desire to give concrete expression to that divine giving, and the Holy Spirit's power that animates the giving of each Person to the other. Every rose, every hair of your head is an event of gift-giving, an ongoing activity of this communion of the three Persons. And that ought to tell us something about how we should treat all creatures. For it means that no creature is just a "thing," a mere object for us to possess. All of us creatures are moments, words, tendernesses exchanged in the trinitarian loving that is God's life.

It is crucial to see here that this is not something extra added on to each creature, some quirky bit of divine stuff secreted within us that the scientists have yet to discover. No, we are all events of God's loving self-giving precisely by being exactly who and what we are, by being truthfully and completely the very creature we each have it in us to be. It is in being ourselves that we are most transparent to God, most symbolic of God's speaking. Suppose your bicycle-riding friend, instead of giving you a box of treasures from all your trips together, had just gone out and bought you a nice box of chocolates. Very tasty, but hardly an authentic sign of your travels together. It is you in all your particular "youness" that is the treasurable gift of God to God. You just as you are, and as you may by grace yet become, are the sign of God's delight.

You can see what I mean just by considering the old philosophical distinction between a blink and a wink. Physically speaking a wink is only a blink, a twitch in the muscles around the eye. But for those who know that at a certain point in time something is *meant* by this particular blink, then this blink is—precisely by being a good blink—also a wink. It has meaning because it has become part of the friendly, secret language between people. By analogy, this is how the universe is "meant" by God. First, it is meant as the divine Persons' loving self-giving to one another; it is part of the gracious language they have chosen to use in order to convey their infinite giving away of life to one another. But creation is also wonderfully "meant" as a symbol, a sacrament, to each and every creature of the loving conversation in which we all participate. We know each other most truly as who and what we are when we become words of God's love to each other. For we are created by divine Love as a gift of love, and we are truest to ourselves when we embody that love in loving one another. We are most fully and authentically ourselves when we have realized that we are the very alphabet of God's grace: the words by which the divine Persons are speaking their love to one another, the vessels by which we are each bearers of the divine. Is it any wonder, then, that if we stand mute, divided, and suspicious before one another, we are called sinners?

Far from excluding God from the cosmos, our growing awareness of the intricacy of things makes us wonder all the more at the kind of meaning God may be using us to express—both to Godself and to us in our relationships with all other creatures. Considered in this way, as part of the language of

God's loving, creation has a powerful momentum toward a goal. We are not, as I have said, just *things*, we are "meanings" tending toward the full flowering of that communion, that infinite conversation which gives us our meaning.

A mid-thirteenth-century poet and spiritual teacher, Hadewijch of Brabant, spoke often of this momentum at the heart of things. For her, all creation expressed in time and space the powerfully surging divine Love, Holy Spirit, ceaselessly drawing the Father and the Son toward the other. In Hadewijch's visionary interpretation, the eternal yearning of the divine Persons toward an ever-deeper unity is, by God's grace, also the fundamental momentum of time and history. The mutual desire of the divine Persons becomes a kind of abyss of love, a vortex of self-giving, that is drawing the whole cosmos toward its consummation. That means that each creature is most fully itself as it fulfills its inherent created tendency to *be* this means of divinely loving speech.

In one of her letters to a religious community of young women, Hadewijch pictures the crucifixion as the vortex of this mutual yearning of the Father and Son. She sees this abyss of divine love in the open mouth, the stretching apart, the wounded side of the crucified Christ, drawing the whole world to himself. Through his wound of love, Jesus draws all creatures into fellowship with one another and so finally into their consummation by participating in God's own life.

> The mouth is open; the arms outstretched; and the rich Heart is ready. That fearful outstretching renders the depth of their souls so deep and so vast that they can never be filled. The fact that God opens himself so wide for them invites

them at all hours to surpass their faculties. For
with his right arm he embraces all his friends,
both heavenly and earthly, in an overflowing
wealth. And on the left side he embraces the
strangers who with naked and scanty faith
come to him for the sake of his friends, so that
there may be fulfilled in them the full and uni-
tive bliss that has never been lacking to him. For
the sake of his good friends and his beloved
ones, he gives the strangers his glory and makes
them all friends of the house.[1]

It is highly significant that, for Hadewijch, one is
never drawn toward creaturely fulfillment in isolation
from others. Jesus, as the "wound," the opening of
God's momentous love in our midst, draws us toward
greater creaturely fulfillment by drawing us toward
each other—strangers and friends are all made
"friends of the house." Furthermore, Jesus tugs us
into creaturely consummation by arousing in us an
ever-deeper love, a love that makes us fit Word-bearers. Christ's outstretching on the cross, says
Hadewijch, stretches apart our own constricted
desires, deepens our own souls so that "they can never
be filled." In this way we are liberated from the lead-
en and pitiful efforts we make to possess each other,
turning one creature after another into an idol. When
Christ's loving is set loose in us we are filled with a
passionate hunger that only God can fulfill. And when
that love animates us, then we can be truthful sacraments to each other.

~ The Author of Freedom
But what if we continually fall short of that love?
What if we are more often not sacraments of divine
love but broken and leaky vessels for each other?

If God has a plan for the whole cosmos, why do things so often seem as if they are reverting to chaos more than moving toward the heaven of divine communion?

One of our problems in thinking about such things is our hunch, based on how things appear, that the more God gets involved in the whole mess the less everyone and everything will be "free" to be whatever it likes. So we maneuver ourselves into an awkward theological corner: either God finally stops dithering around out there and takes charge of our mess, or else we must grimly knuckle down to righteousness and straighten ourselves out. I hope by now you will sense that this is not really how things are. The mystery of creation does not point us toward a God who must either make puppets out of us to make things "better" or abandon us to give us our "freedom." After all, do we really think God gives us our freedom by stepping out of the universe and leaving us to get on with it on our own?

Such a view would be a particularly insidious kind of idolatry. It pictures God as a kind of bullying parent whose presence interferes with us growing up into truly free adults but who sometimes evaporates so that we can become at last who we really are. For those who are not so lucky, the oppressive parent idol is too powerful and they go through life alternately cringing, whining, and blaming mean old "God" for how things have turned out. Unfortunately, many people who call themselves atheists belong to the first category—the nasty idol they managed to "grow out of" as a teenager is really the living God. Even more unfortunately, many people who have never realized that they are in bondage to an idol are active and painfully vociferous Christians!

Now let's consider what it would mean for any of us to be free. Surely part of the definition is that we are free when a) we are being our true selves and b) nothing is making us do something against our will. Of course, various forces are always contributing to our life and action, but we count some of them as getting in the way of our freedom (as when my one-year-old gets a painful grip on my ear) and others as fostering our freedom (as when the same one-year-old gives me a big hug when I get home from work). And we tend to distinguish between these two by saying that some things work against our freedom by preventing us from discovering and being our true selves, and other things contribute to our freedom by deepening and strengthening our self-understanding and our ability to live that out.

The bossy parent idol derives from a common experience of growing up in which we learn to be ourselves because, at appropriate points, our parents stepped back and "gave" us the freedom to find our own limits and abilities. But our parents, no matter how big a role they may have played in our lives, are just like us—other beings of the universe. And this is exactly what God is not. To interfere with my freedom, the interfering one has to be another item in the universe along with me. God is no such item. The mystery of creation lets me know God as the One who is not only the source of my existing, but who causes me to exist precisely by giving me the power to be me, the unique self that I am becoming.

To become our true selves we all had at a certain point to become "independent" of our parents, because freedom meant freedom *from them.* The exact opposite is the case with respect to God. Being "independent" from God does not mean having the freedom to discover and be myself, it means ceasing to exist. God is the ever-present *source* of my freedom to be me. God brings my freedom about by giving me myself to become. The real problem is not that God's presence gets in the way of my freedom, but that my distorted understanding of myself prevents me from acting freely.

Have you ever found yourself making inane conversation at a party and then later felt disgusted with yourself? We often pretend to be things that we are not, perhaps because we are insecure about how we will be perceived, or because we do not like the person we think we really are. Our world is full of situations that garble and distort our sense of self. Instead of hearing God's delighted call to me as a beloved child, for example, perhaps I can hear only an abusive parent's message that I am ugly or unlovable, or the advertisers' pitch that the real me is only discovered by buying this kind of car or that kind of sweater. The mystery of creation beckons us to discover the truth about ourselves by entering into the loving self-giving that is pulsing us into existence at every moment. It tells us that we are most free—the bravest, gladdest, kindest, and holiest we could ever be—precisely by bearing that self-giving love to each other. That is the pattern and meaning of life, which is inherent in every fibre of our existence. We exist as the language of God's trinitarian life, and insofar as we are liberated to be this loving speech of God, we are free at last and true to ourselves.

The wonderful Anglican scholar and detective novelist Dorothy Sayers drew many of these themes together in her book on the Trinity, *The Mind of the Maker*.[2] Throughout this book, Sayers draws on her own experience as an author to help us think about our relationship as creatures to the divine Trinity. First of all, she makes it abundantly clear how intimately

God is present to us as the very source of our freedom; just as an author is the source and basis of her characters' existence and freedom, so we would become pale prototypes of persons were God's mind somehow to "withdraw" from us. The more intimately the Author is present in the least details of our being, the more alive and lively we become—not as stick figures, mere mouthpieces, but as persons with a vitality and character uniquely their own. It is only the mediocre author whose characters are all insipid automatons, merely bobbing along through the hoops set before them. By contrast, an author who has really invested herself in her characters feels that they have a life of their own, which is all the more real for the close interest and care she continually lavishes upon them.

All of which brings us back to the question at the beginning of this section: namely, if God is such a great creator, why is the world in such a mess? One of the usual answers to this question says that of course God *could* simply swoop in and tidy everything up, but that would interfere with our freedom, so to preserve this freedom God stays out of our muddle. Yet we have seen that, far from remaining distant from all the griefs and sorrows in the world, God is intimately present in all the creatures, both those who suffer and those who cause suffering for others. But God is not present in the same way in each case. For as the immediate giver of existence to all being, God is immediately present to everything that exists. As we have also seen, however, not every creature is living out the gift of its existence with equal clarity.

Suppose, for example, I decide that I can fulfill myself most fully by robbing banks. Suppose further, as is very likely, that in the course of this nefarious activity I injure other people in order to get my way. Now God is not quite off the hook here because God is still giving me my existence moment by moment, including those moments when I am stealing other people's money. The problem is that the language of creation has broken down in my case; I am no longer able to hear the Word that God is speaking in causing me to be. Have you ever listened to a five-year-old sing Sousa marches through a kazoo during a very long car ride? With the best will in the world, after about ten or twenty minutes very little of the rousing spirit of Sousa's music will be entrancing to your ears. Even after about five minutes, I find that all I can hear is painful and, dare I say it, increasingly irritating noise. By analogy, if I become a bank robber, we could say that instead of hearing the music of creation clearly—the loving language of the divine Persons one to another—I have begun to hear it through the nightmarish kazoo of a broken and sinful world where we only seem to fit in by being an even more vicious kazoo player than the next person. Sin is no longer knowing the truth of who I have it in me to be, no longer wanting to know, and being unwilling and unable to act like the person God called me to be.

It was St. Paul's view that we all *ought* to have known very well what God was saying to us in the creation of the universe, particularly in loving us into being. But because humankind has gone its way grasping after equality with God instead of receiving it lovingly from the Giver, "they became futile in their thinking, and their senseless minds were darkened. Claiming to be wise, they became fools" (Romans 1:21-22). We now live in a world in which it can be hard to hear the real truth about ourselves, and insofar as we lose touch with that true self, we fall into a kind of unreality; we are pseudo-Words to each other, or worse. Creation, us included, is God's loving speech, but we now need a special gift in order to hear and to be the bearers of that Word.

It was partly for this reason that the early Christians so loved the idea that, in the Genesis story, humanity was created on the "sixth day" of the week. Humanity is that part of the creation which was supposed to give harmony to all the other earthly creatures, to articulate for them the Word that God was speaking through all. Thus humanity was to be the mediator between the earthly creation and that even more articulate realm of the heavenly creatures—pure intelligences, angels or messengers—of God's loving self-giving. But humanity has forsaken its role and no longer gives voice to every creature under heaven. So the early Christians were fascinated by the fact that Jesus was also crucified on a Friday, the "sixth day" of the week. In Christ, our humanity struggled through the blare and bitterness of the world's sin to hear the truth of his identity as God's Beloved. And finally, on the sixth day, he *consummated* that humanity by continuing to love, to *be* the Word of God's love, even incarnate in the maw of the world's deafening babble.

In the next chapter, on the mystery of revelation, we will consider how God works to heal our distorted hearing and speaking, how God restores to us our identity as Word-bearers by drawing us into the self-disclosure of the Word in Jesus, and how finally God frees our lives to speak boldly of the divine love by bringing our babble through the cross to Pentecost. Revelation, I will suggest, is not something God "adds on" to the speech of creation. No, revelation is how creation learns to speak anew; it is creation passing through Christ's death into resurrection life.

Chapter Four

The Voice of God

The Mystery of Revelation

> You never enjoy the world aright, till you see how a sand exhibiteth the wisdom and power of God.
>
> —*Thomas Traherne*

When I was a child, I would sometimes get out of my bed, go over to the window, and listen into the darkness—that sound of the wind in the trees was so beautiful to me, so fresh and strong. I always sensed something vastly, inexpressibly good in the whispering of the leaves, the surging of the wind, even the aching whine of bare branches in a winter storm. I can still remember, above all, the summer nights when the breeze would dance all the evocative scents of the heavy air through my window. I would stand by the window and try, in that innocently serious way only open to children, to hear what the wind was saying in all its fragrances and rustlings.

On special nights, when the wind was just right, I could hear real music. Our neighbor was a pianist, and though I have no idea what she used to play, I remember the wind carrying her music across her

yard and into my window for me to hear. It was as if
the wind itself had selected these broken snatches of
melody, rising and falling cadences fading in and out
on the humid night air. Sometimes I imagined that
this was the *real* sound of the wind itself, playing in
the leaves, letting me hear for once the silent music of
its own life—as though the wind had a hidden har-
monics all its own that I could sometimes sense and
sometimes only wish to hear.

Such an awareness of the tingling, living, *speaking*
quality of the world, of its inner music, its sacramental glory—all this was never far from our forebears.
The wonderfully imaginative seventeenth-century
Anglican priest and poet Thomas Traherne suggested
that we could never fully understand the world until
we sensed the divine voice that speaks the world *and*
us into being:

> You never enjoy the world aright, till you see
> how a sand exhibiteth the wisdom and power of
> God: And prize in everything the service which
> they do you, by manifesting His glory and
> goodness to your Soul, far more than the visible
> beauty on their surface, or the material services
> they can do your body.[1]

Traherne's point is that the bounty and glory of the
world may work wonders for our bodily needs and
our yearning for beauty. Even more important, however, these gifts to us are also signs of the intimate
love and goodness of our Creator. Like my experience
of the wind, the whole creation bears within it the
hidden music of the Creator's loving communion with
us. In a very real sense, Traherne suggests, it is the
intimacy of God's self-giving presence in all creation
that is its greatest blessing to us. The stars that delight
our sight and the water that quenches our thirst are

sacramental signs of the deeper blessing of God's communion with us—a communion God begins to establish by giving us stars to marvel at and water to drink.

God's universe is a whispering, speaking universe. Every creature is part of this alphabet, the language God uses to speak to us—including the way, in acts of great love or simple human kindness, we sometimes become a powerful word to one another of God's presence. In creating the universe this way, God invests each creature with a marvelous potential for glory, a whispered destiny of great hope. For the miracle is that we are each not less but more ourselves by fulfilling our potential as God's speech. The wetness of water, its power to cleanse and purify, to drown and to give life, is never more apparent than in baptism. Likewise, bread and wine are more than daily food when in every eucharist they become for us the bread of life and the cup of salvation, the body and blood of Christ.

This vision of reality itself as the revelation of God's presence was a central feature of Christianity for most of its history. Realizing this can help us to make sense of what we mean when we talk about "revelation" today. For in the more recent past our vision has suffered from a nearly fatal narrowing of what it would mean for God to "speak" and for us to "know" or understand this speaking. When earlier generations of Christians considered the universe, they saw it as an ordered cosmos, whose very laws were the speech of the divine Word. Every harmony of nature was a reflection of the moment-by-moment self-expression *(Logos)* or Word of God, come in the fullness of time to particular expression in a baby crying in Bethlehem, a man crying out on Calvary.

The fact that John's gospel speaks of the Word of God becoming flesh in Jesus was a miracle to earlier Christians, but it was *not* incomprehensible. For this same Word was also becoming "flesh," so to speak, in every fibre of creation, filling the universe with life and meaning, glory and purpose. Even more astonishing, the whole creation, since it has been brought into being by this Speaking, is in a mysterious way *designed* for communion with the self-giving Word of God.

Have you ever tried something completely new, and been astonished at the sense of fulfillment it gave you? Maybe your first roller-coaster ride, or the first time you ate real homemade applesauce—or the first time you fell in love? "Oh, my goodness, I was *made* for this!" you feel like shouting. Well, in a far deeper and more wonderful way, the whole creation is *made* for participation in God's Speaking. Every blade of grass, every mountain range, every act of human loving is brought to fulfillment as it is taken up into the language of God's giving life.

Christians have long pondered the fact that since the eternal Word is the image of God, and humankind in particular is created in the image of God (as in Genesis 1:26), we can see how apt human existence is to become in a very special way the language in which the Word might come to speech, become flesh. This is a point we will consider further in the next chapter on the mystery of the Word's incarnation as Jesus. Just for the moment, though, let me try to show how our humanity helps us to understand the whole idea of revelation more deeply.

Suppose you were gifted with incredible talents as a composer. The shining of the stars, the vastness of mountains, the exhilaration of a child rolling down a hill—all flow through you onto paper as musical notation. But you live among beings who sense all air vibrations as noise, but never as music. The strange markings you put on paper are puzzled over by the scientists as unintelligible, frowned at as very poor art by your friends, and simply ignored as useless curiosities by everyone else. There are no musical instruments because no one ever would have dreamed of inventing them; and when you try to sing your music, people just comfort you as someone in terrible pain or lead you away where no one will have to be exposed to your odd behavior.

But over time some people, perhaps a bit odd themselves, come to visit you. You sing to them, you teach them to keep rhythm with their hands and feet, and gradually, without realizing it, they begin to notice a strange phenomenon. Out of the chaotic buzz of noise they notice some sounds that are patterned, intentional, and expressive. They discover music! The confused welter of noises distills into a whole new dimension as they learn to *perceive* music, to recognize and respond in delight to this new dimension in life. In a very real sense, these people developed the power to experience music because you sang it to life in them.

The point of this analogy is to suggest that through the whole history of life on earth God has been speaking and singing and loving the creatures into one new dimension of life after another: motion, sensation, hearing, sight, instinctual drives, and so on. But only very recently has one species emerged that has the dimension of choosing to risk falling in love. We are not always very *good* at loving, but we have been lovingly given the *capacity*. Through this we have been given, therefore, a glimpse of a whole new dimension of being, a dimension of freely given, personal love for another that is far more than a mere instinctual drive.

The patterns of human life may not always reveal much of that risky, self-giving kind of love, but they are able to express it; our human ways of being with each other are *made* for the expression of a certain kind of freedom and love. Human speech, human fellowship, human loving are like letters of an alphabet designed for a language whose marvels of expression are hard for us to bear but are nonetheless the very making of our life. The language is spoken in acts of healing, of repentance and reconciliation, of a last terrible betrayal and a self-giving love that loves until the end. It is the language of Christ's life and death, his resurrection and ascension, that breaks out jubilantly if awkwardly on the feast of Pentecost.

Just as the friends in my analogy above who learned to hear music by listening to you sing are going to be especially well suited to sing and dance to your music, so humankind is especially suited to know and recognize the divine love that has aroused and awakened and called it to life in us. The whole universe echoes with this love, but humanity can hear it and recognize it. In being created as loving persons, we have been given a cherishable—if easily distorted—aptitude for hearing and embodying the loving personhood of God. The Anglican theologian William Temple put it this way: "The personal God can only be adequately revealed in and through persons; but then such revelation must be distorted by any defects in the persons through whom it comes."[2] Archbishop Temple suggests that the beauty of the heavens is perfect, and in that sense it is a fitting testimony to its maker. However, we do not assume the stars shine because they desire to burn themselves up giving light to the universe; rather, they shine "impersonally" in a more or less mechanical fashion. Because they lack intentionality, they cannot with complete adequacy express the free, personal, loving reality whom we name God. By contrast, as human persons we do have this capacity to choose to risk ourselves in loving self-giving for another.

What I am suggesting is that the universe is "intel-ligible," able to be understood and known in the way that intelligent speech can. Men and women are entrusted with the special tasks of recognizing that Word, sensing it intuitively, and also responding to it. For the Word does not simply come forth from the Father, but also seeks to praise the Father, to return thanks on behalf of all creation, and to do so within and by means of our life together, the new life of dis-cipleship and mutual service. So there is an inherent harmony between the universe, as the work of God's self-communication, and human life as interpreting and giving thanks for the gift of that sacramental presence of God. Both the universe as a whole and human life as a responsive and loving part of the uni-verse are being "spoken" by the same Word.

The problem is that instead of giving ourselves over to those tasks of repentance and discipleship, in the west we have become preoccupied with a different question: that of the certainty or even the possibility of any human knowledge of God at all. Instead of realizing that our problem in hearing God aright has to do with sin, we have become convinced that the whole business of revelation hinges on whether the very idea of God speaking can make sense. Disobedience and infidelity to God make us increas-ingly insensitive to God's call to us in the prophets of Israel and the gospel of Christ, to say nothing of God's loving desire to address us in creation itself and in our relationships with one another. But since the time of early modernity (ca. 1600) there has been an almost irresistible tendency in Christian theology to sidestep

the question of sin and instead to label revelation as
the problem in and of itself. That allows us to worry
about other questions instead—important questions,
of course, but not at the heart of the matter. It strikes
me as a little fishy that these discussions of revelation
tend to avoid any consideration of the very first thing
Jesus says to us from a gospel: "The time is fulfilled,
and the kingdom of God has come near; repent, and
believe in the good news" (Mark 1:15).

~ How Do You Know? A Modern Problem

As we seek to understand the Christian mystery of
revelation, we need to consider how our understanding has been influenced by the peculiarly modern concern for "certainty"—a concern we often express by
asking, "How do you know?" How do we know that
God is speaking to us? How can we be sure of what is
"said"? What would it mean for us to hear and
respond to God's self-communication, to understand
the Word being spoken to us in the wind of a summer
night or by a child's playing or through the loss of one
much loved? For generations of Christians, "knowing"
reality in this deep sense has not meant something
that we know by reading a book or by looking
through a microscope, but by learning to practice
fidelity to Christ. By sharing in Jesus' ministry of reconciling love, Christians have found growing in themselves those habits of heart and intuitions of soul that
draw them into God's own knowing of God, the
Word's knowing of the Father. In other words, for
most of Christian history, *understanding* reality has
been integrally connected with *loving* it.

By the later Middle Ages, this sense of the meaningfulness of the universe as the language of God's
Word, a language learned and spoken and understood
by loving, had begun to change. It was supplanted by

the idea that we can better magnify God's majesty by counting divine action as wholly inscrutable to human understanding. Late medieval thinkers like William of Ockham insisted that everything exists solely by the act of the divine will. To conceive of the universe as the unfolding of God's loving meaning in time and space, was, in this view, to subject the divine will to human norms and human understanding. The universe, nature, and the world do not resonate with divine purpose, but assert divine power, and the mind has no business speculating about that.

Notice what this means. First, it means that the mind is no longer related to the universe as part of an integral, cosmic whole, and so nature and mind become mutually opaque, separate and closed off from each other. For the ancients, "knowing" was an activity in which the mind participates (ultimately by loving) in the life of the "known," but for us, "knowing" is not an act of communion but a private, individual act of cognition. And since "knowing" is now a private act, it becomes increasingly hard for us to see how sin could have implications for how or what I can know. If knowing is no longer a form of communion that can be harmed and distorted by sin, it has become no more than a private experience of my own, subject only to the laws of human cognition.

Second, nature itself is now unintelligible, without any divinely bestowed meaning. That means our task is not to interpret and respond to God's glory, but to stand over against nature and to impart to it whatever meaning we can. Nature, in other words, becomes more and more an object not for our reverence and thanksgiving, but for our analysis and control.

By the time of early modern thinkers like Francis Bacon in the late sixteenth and early seventeenth centuries, knowledge is described explicitly as the "dissection" of nature; we must put nature upon the rack and torture it in order to pry loose its secrets. In this emerging scientific method truth can only be known by the reduction of reality to its most elemental components. In the seventeenth century the philosopher René Descartes would carry this reductionism further: the new attempt to model reality not according to its own form and beauty, but according to mathematics. The only certainty (and Descartes was frantically in pursuit of certainty) is the pure and pristine certainty of the mathematical formula. Henceforth all that is concrete—tornadoes, music, the human mind—are to be reduced to abstract propositions. In this view, reality is either reducible to numbers or it is entirely negligible. One late Renaissance thinker, foreseeing the effects of this new "method" on our manner of knowing, commented grimly: "Those whose hands have ground the majestic beauty of nature into disembodied concepts, horrible abstractions, and empty subtleties have terribly flattened and diluted philosophy."[3] Today we accept that modern scientific method is useful; but we also know that as a *way* of knowing it has its limits. Reducing a flower to its components, to compounds, to elements, and finally to subatomic particles negates the importance of being entranced by its fragrance or mesmerized by its beauty, which are the best ways of really knowing it as a flower.

In Descartes's day, everybody, including most forward-thinking theologians, assumed that if Christian thought was not to be relegated to half-life in a museum, it would have to be reformulated in clear, distinct, propositions. These propositions would have to be either universally acceptable to all reasonable persons or else, as a fall-back position, inerrantly inspired or infallibly taught. In short, the model of the scientific method of knowing and its disdain for anything less than certainty set down deep roots in modern Christianity. Interestingly, today both fundamentalists on one side and revisionist liberal Christians on the other remain locked into this early modern scientific approach to knowing. Revelation itself remains for them either encapsulated in tidy, numbered propositions or reduced to whatever domain of science they tend to favor most, such as psychology.

As I have been suggesting, however, there are many other ways of knowing what is real, living, and true. In these other ways of knowing, certainty is not something we exhaust ourselves to achieve, but something God provides. Revelation is not what we learn on our own about God, as though God were an especially complex lab specimen. Instead, revelation is the mystery of God "undoing" us, taking our side against ourselves, and making us worthy to stand in divine fellowship. Revelation is simply God giving God away to God, and including us for the sheer joy of it.

Revelation is what God's own life of trinitarian communion looks like when we are drawn into it. Its reliability and "certainty" are always miraculous because revelation happens not through distant observation, but through participation. Revelation happens when people are rescued from slavery in Egypt, when they discover their very lives are being put to death and brought to life in companionship with Christ. Revelation is not something we can cut up into pieces and certify on the grounds that it makes sense, or fits in fairly well with other things we all know, or is not too far out of touch with the latest theories of science. Revelation *does* make sense, but that is the result of God letting the world in on the eternal sense and meaning at the heart of everything. Revelation is God drawing the world back to the purpose for its creation—fellowship with God—*and* giving us a glimpse of the whole unbelievable business while it happens. And that means revelation is going to involve something happening to *us*.

ᦔ Revelation is Jesus

Think how, as you come to spend more and more time with a person, you come to know more deeply who she is. That is only possible because at the same time *you* are being changed by your friendship with her— sometimes brought up short, sometimes delighted, sometimes wounded in your pride, sometimes healed and forgiven. All these changes in you are the means by which you come to know your friend more and more, because knowing someone in that intimate way is only possible through a process of transformation and growth—sometimes painful, always unsettling— by which you and your friend come to share life together. Similarly, revelation happens when, by the miracle of God's grace, we are brought to share in the love of the Trinity. As we know, such sharing is risky for us in the world *we* have made. God's giving-life-in-you (usually called "grace") leads you out of the self others have made for you by their anger or their possessiveness, and it tugs you out of the life you have settled into as a way of hiding from what God longs for you to be. It sends you into soup kitchens and night shelters, to hospital bedsides and communion rails, it exhausts you and gives you life, it gets you crucified and yet raises you into Life itself.

The gospels are full of these personal transformations, people whose lives are changed far beyond the simple bit of help or healing or whatever it was that led them to Jesus in the first place. One of our hymns expresses this transformation well:

Contented, peaceful fishermen,
before they ever knew
the peace of God that filled their hearts
brimful, and broke them too.
Young John who trimmed the flapping sail,
homeless, in Patmos died.
Peter, who hauled the teeming net,
head-down was crucified.[4]

The words may seem sentimental, yet I expect the reality was anything but—the awesome wonder of the gift of new life, the discovery and confession of one's own failures, the inescapable tide of Christ's ministry pulling them out beyond all the known moorings of the life they had thought to live on their own terms. And what is so unsettling about revelation is that God seems to insist on luring us into the whole act: we are shocked that God seems to reveal exactly who God is by rescuing us. Jesus, Christians believe, is the Word, the self-disclosure of God, but this Word is spoken in the ever-expanding community of those whose own lives have begun to "speak" the same language. Jesus *is* himself, acting as God's Word—by drawing us into his own life, and death, and resurrection.

Austin Farrer, a twentieth-century Anglican theologian, captures this mutuality of the Word:

[Jesus] needed a mother to smile at him, a father to talk to him, if he was ever going to be a man. Without Mary and Joseph he wouldn't have been anyone on earth. The divine life came to earth in Jesus, he was the heart and centre of it: but the divine life could not live or act in Jesus alone. The divine life had to use his parents, his kindred and his friends, to make Jesus a man; and had to use his disciples and associ-

ates to keep him being a man; for we cannot go
on being human, any more than we can get to
be human, without other people.... What is a
teacher, without pupils or disciples to pull the
wisdom out of his heart? And what can a
Saviour be, without souls to attach to God, by
attaching them to himself? Jesus could only be
Jesus, by having Peter, James and John to be
himself with.[5]

The divine life is itself communal life, a loving life of
being one-with-another. If we had not fallen into sin,
perhaps God could have revealed the divine life simply
by stretching out divine arms in welcome, but in the
world we have made, this stretching out of welcome
and love comes to be a stretching out upon the hard
wood of the cross. Revelation, in other words, is by
God's great mercy not separable for us from our
transformation. God can only really show us who
God is by transforming us as fit partakers of God's
life.

This tells us something very important. Revelation
as a mutual process confirms my hunch that it is not
something that happens "out there." It is certainly an
event, but an event that refuses to keep apart from
those among whom it takes place; it reaches out as an
infant latching onto a mother's finger, a teacher
molding the minds and hearts of students, a shepherd
pulling a stubborn sheep out of a cleft. We can only
know revelation by letting it work within us the mystery of redemption.

There are, of course, a wide range of views about
how revelation takes place. One end of the spectrum
holds that revelation is purely "objective." The divinely inspired events and scriptural accounts of those
events are seen as entirely objective truths, pristine

and revelatory quite apart from whether anyone happens to notice them, understand them, or be changed by them. At the other end is the view that revelation is primarily "subjective." It is a shift in a person's own understanding of reality that might be occasioned by some historical event, a biblical account, a parable or, just as easily, a visit to your high school reunion or drinking a diet cola. The *occasion* for the transformation is immaterial: what matters is the new way of thinking and living. In this view, whether Jesus himself actually existed or not is not nearly so important as whether the stories about him gave rise to a new understanding of life—"authentic existence" or "deeper life." So Jesus and the whole history of Israel are handy though dispensable visual aids to help us recognize something that is really already available within us if we could just get in touch with it. Obviously, I am caricaturing the second extreme, but only because I think it has a certain currency in contemporary culture. In this view, revelation could never be good *news* about a change in the history of the world, but only a helpful *reminder* of something pretty nice that was always true anyway.

The problem with the first, objective extreme stems from its fundamental assumption: the God who is revealed in the mystery of revelation can be adequately revealed *apart* from redeeming us. It presupposes that we can know God's inner life without becoming part of it through healing and redemption. Imagine if I said to you, "I'll show you what a real party is like!" and then gave you the blood pressure readings for all the guests. A party, like dancing, is something that I can only "show" you by bringing you to the party itself, filling a glass with drink and a belly with laughter and turning unknown faces into friends.

The self-disclosure of God cannot take place fully in one "historical event," a bit of the past that is over and gone. Instead, revelation is an event that continues to stand open before us, so what happened between Jesus and his first followers is, by the power of God the Holy Spirit, still happening in our midst. The events of God's self-disclosure in creation and in the Exodus and in the coming of Jesus do take place *in time*, but because they take place by the hand of God, they still beckon us to be transformed forever by our sharing in the Exodus, the words of the prophets, and above all the paschal mystery itself. So the fact that God is revealed precisely by *rescuing* us in Christ helps us to understand what revelation is: it is God coming to find us and bring us home.

The fact that revelation takes this form also tells us something about who *God* is. The fact that revelation only happens by catching us up into the process shows us that the divine life is a communal life, a sharing life. God's life, in other words, is trinitarian: the eternal Father loves the Son, the Son in turn loves the Father, and "it is into this eternal exchange of love between Jesus and the Father that we are taken up, this exchange of love that we call the Holy Spirit."[6]

∽ Revelation, Holy Scripture, and the Church's Life

How are we to interpret the scriptures and the church's life, therefore, in light of what we have learned about revelation so far? The central Christian conviction is that in Jesus of Nazareth we have been found and embraced by this one Word of God, that in Jesus he has come among us. This means that in Christ we will find the clue to recognize and respond to God's Speaking in every time and every place. As our Eucharistic Prayer B puts it:

> We give thanks to you, O God, for the goodness
> and love which you have made known to us in
> creation; in the calling of Israel to be your peo-
> ple; in your Word spoken through the prophets;
> and above all in the Word made flesh, Jesus,
> your Son. (BCP 368)

All the other ways in which the Word speaks, we
could say, are extensions, whispers, and hints of the
Word's most concentrated and direct speech: the life,
death, resurrection, and ascension of Jesus of
Nazareth.

When some scholars talk about "the historical
Jesus" and whether he actually said or did this or that
in the gospels, how are such scholars understanding
the mystery of revelation itself? Revelation happens, I
have been suggesting, because of the *way* Jesus goes
about being who he is: by weaving the lives of his disciples into his, drawing them and us in to abide in his
relationship with the Father. The life of the communities that grow up around him are also the expression
of his own life through their teaching and worship
and caring for one another. So to say there is a great
difference between the "Jesus of history" and the
"Christ of faith" is to betray a considerable misunder-
standing of revelation, one that is characteristic of our
day. The Word does not become incarnate as Jesus
only to hold back priggishly from ongoing *embodiment* in the church's life and teaching.

The point is that the church's life and teaching are
themselves called into being by revelation, by God's
Word. Jesus' historical life is the embodiment of his
identity as God's Word, but—and this is the crucial
issue—his historical life is not the *limit* of his identity.
For his identity and mission as God's Word is to pass
into the very depths of human suffering and grief,

into death itself, to pass into our lives and raise them up in him, weaving them into his joyous offering of himself to the Father. Jesus' identity as God's Word means that he cannot be *captured* in any historical reconstruction, like an archaeological exhibit displayed in a glass case. God speaks to us not by standing still, an interesting figure of the past, safely cordoned off from us by history; God's Word comes to us in the messy, gloriously impossible realities of existence that Jesus has brought into being as his continuing life, confronting us each day with our own mission and call to discipleship. Jesus does not hold himself aloof from the confused and occasionally corrupted life of his Body; God the Holy Spirit works within this communal life of Christ, bringing it to judgment, repentance, and fidelity to its mission by immersing it ever more deeply into the Lord's own dying and rising.

We see this happening every Sunday. All over the world the Holy Spirit calls Christ's people together, remembering his Body, nourishing it with word and sacraments, calling it back to conformity with the mind of Christ. In the eucharist we pray that God the Holy Spirit would bring our gifts of bread and wine, and our very selves, into the offering of Jesus. Christ draws us into his exchange of love with the Father, takes our fears and confusions and great desires and draws them into his own speaking. As the choir member moves to the lectern to read the second lesson, her mind still teeming with all the confusion of getting the kids ready for church, her life itself with all its difficult reality becomes the speaking voice of God. The truth of who we are is not lost when we participate in the event of revelation, but is brought in touch with a still deeper truth: that we are loved and that our fulfillment will come in living and serving Christ together.

This speaking of the Word in our life as church is clarified and corrected by the Word's speaking in the scriptures. The Bible, we could say, like the church's sacraments, discipline, and teaching, is the vehicle for the Word's revelation. The reality of this is, of course, often obscured for us. Prophets and apostles have been known to resist their calling in all kinds of ways, and we all know how inadequate a given sermon, annual parish meeting, or communion anthem can be. The Word's speech in scripture or the church's life can also be difficult for us to hear because of our own hardness of heart, perhaps because of sins done to us and wounds suffered, perhaps because of our failures to love and grow in ways that open us to God's speech. We should not be too worried when these things happen, just ready to repent, trusting that God has not baptized us into the drama of Christ's Body only to forsake us when we stumble over some of our lines.

Only Jesus himself *is* the Word of God as such. Scripture and the church are both modes of his speaking, and each has special strengths as expressions of Jesus' life. The Bible is written; it is a powerfully crystallized form of the Word's speaking. It is a canon of scripture (a Greek word meaning a unit of measure), and it has the power to speak to people who are wandering in darkness and have lost all proportion in life. The Bible judges and cries out against the church's abdication of its duty, whether for introspection or for traditionalism or for idolization of contemporary culture. Conversely, the living community of Jesus' followers has the power to bring the words of scripture to life, to enact the promises of God in its life together through faith in them in ways that can speak to every time and place. So scripture as the *written* Body of the Word and the church as the *eucharistic* Body of the Word must constantly be united and held together.

✓ Reading Scripture

So how do we interpret scripture as God's Word? Perhaps we could look again at two extemes as a way to find the middle path. One view that is associated with fundamentalism, whether Protestant or Roman Catholic, would be to *equate* the words of scripture with the Word of God. This view would insist that every biblical phrase is equally and inerrantly God's Word. If we applied this to the biblical testimony regarding the resurrection of Jesus, it would hold that the biblical reports are just that: literal, historical accounts.

The other extreme, associated with liberal revisions of Christianity, insists that the Bible is written in myths and symbols, evocative but primitive cultural expressions of universal experiences common to many religions. These myths and symbols are jumping-off points for our own personal quests for inner meaning and deep truth. If we cling to them as they are, then they will not only become idols, but barriers to our self-realization and personal freedom. Thus in this view the biblical accounts of the resurrection are symbolic; a mythological picture-language for saying that the disciples came to have a new faith, or that love is stronger than death, or that spring always comes again. But they do not tell us anything about something that happened to *Jesus*.

In many ways, these two extremes are not so different from the views that classical Anglican thinkers like Richard Hooker had to steer between in Tudor England, one of Anglicanism's most formative periods. Today the challenge is still to find the living middle way. Hans Frei, an Episcopal priest and for many years a professor at Yale, spent much of his later life painstakingly developing such a perspective. I would say that Frei's understanding of the strange history of biblical interpretation in the modern era has come to be recognized as a watershed.

Frei's theory, put very simply, is that from about the time of Bacon and Descartes, biblical scholars began to lose sight of what kind of a text they were actually working with. They misunderstood the Bible's "genre." Imagine, for example, reading a poem as if it were completely autobiographical. Perhaps something of the poet's own life would be revealed in the poem, but if you tried to make every verse and phrase tell you something about the poet's childhood or debilitating struggle with disease, for example, you would not appreciate it as poetry. In fact, you might even get frustrated and say what a terribly poor autobiography it is!

Frei's point is that, almost without realizing it, scholars began to do that with scripture. They treated it as though it belonged either to the genre of literal historical record—in which case conservatives claimed it was a reliable record and liberals that it was faulty—or to the genre of ancient myth. If the latter, then it was not so different from the myths of other prescientific cultures, whose meaning could only be rescued if we looked beyond the text to universal truths of human experience.

Frei's studies of the history of biblical interpretation led him to believe that neither of these approaches to the Bible worked. For what we have in the Bible is something far more like a sacrament. Its outward and visible forms—stories, prophecy, poetry, letters—are the revelation of God's invisible and ungraspable presence.

Above I suggested that revelation takes place as God speaks the divine life through different forms of embodiment, from creation and history to the incarnate form of the Word as Jesus, and from there to the resurrection life of Christ poured out through the church in Pentecost, and living still in eucharist and scripture. Revelation is the *whole* sweep. The unfolding process of revelation cannot be captured in any given moment, and yet each form it takes (in this case, the Bible) is crucial to the ongoing encounter of humanity with God. The biblical witness, in other words, tells of prior historical events, but does not stop there; it moves on to encounters of the community with God today and mediates that encounter.

So, for example, Frei would argue that the resurrection stories do have as their subject the miracle of the bodily resurrection of Jesus and not just a "resurrection" of the disciples' faith. The miracle of Jesus' resurrection is a real event, even though the reality of the resurrection is beyond our grasp. The text is not like a photograph, Frei argues, because what these stories depict is not only "fragmentary and confusing," but a series of miraculous events that are "unique, incomparable, and impenetrable—in short, the abiding mystery of the union of the divine with the historical, for our salvation from sin and death."[7]

Frei is saying, in other words, that we cannot use the language and imagery of the Bible to get back to some objective underlying history, just as we cannot take them as particularly fine symbols or metaphors for universal truths. Rather, the biblical language is *itself* the place of encounter. As human language it could never tell us everything about these particular historical events because Jesus' death and resurrection have infinite and eternal significance. Nevertheless, the biblical language *is* adequate and absolutely necessary for our journeying into the mystery. It becomes the new lens through which we begin to recognize and respond to all the myriad ways God is with us.

The momentum of God's Word draws the biblical language into being; it also confronts us, drawing us into the presence of God ourselves. Of course it is helpful to learn about the historical circumstances behind the biblical texts, just as it is helpful to consider how the Bible often speaks to hopes and fears, anxieties and aspirations that find expression in many different cultures. But the meaningfulness and truth of the scriptures, like the meaningfulness and truth of the church's life, does not rest finally in either the history behind the text or existential feelings beyond the text, but in God's will to speak to us by means of the text. The mystery of revelation is at work in the Bible, in the church's life and teaching, in the scriptures of our own lives, precisely because in all of them the one Word of God, whom we meet definitively as Jesus, wills to speak. The miracle is that he calls, and heals, and claims our words and our lives to become the very language by which he speaks most intimately in our midst.

Chapter Five

The Humanity of God

The Mystery of the Incarnation

> I slept, but my heart was awake.
> Listen! My beloved is knocking.
>   *The Song of Solomon 5:2*

"Hush now. Go to sleep."
"But I can't. I'm not sleepy!"
"I can see that, but it's late, and I'm tired."
"Please, just one more song, just one, please!"
"All right, but that's *it* then, okay?"
"Okay, I promise."

E very night children all over the world are so exhil-
arated, so enthused by the sheer liveliness of life
that they cannot bear to relinquish it, not even for
sleep. There are moments, of course, when adults
(exhausted as we usually are) can also rediscover
something of that passion of our childhood, moments
when we are awakened by something that truly stirs
us and captures our imagination. We could even say
that those moments of rekindled passion are signs of
the deep current of desire that animates our lives: the
desire to explore freely, to understand, to create and

plant, to build and sometimes to destroy, and above all to love and be loved. It will be almost impossible to understand much of the church's thinking about Jesus unless we talk about desire, a deep stirring and awakening to fullness of life.

～ The Desire that Becomes You

It may seem odd to begin a chapter on the Incarnàtion by talking about desire, but this is really the starting point. So let's begin there, because it will make thinking about the Incarnation a bit easier. As I mentioned in chapter four, understanding Jesus is not like someone in a lab coat probing an inanimate specimen under a microscope, for the one whom we seek to understand is, Christians believe, very much alive and with us now more than ever. In fact, even as I write these words and as you read them, Jesus is, by the power of the Holy Spirit, with us both. I admit to feeling slightly unnerved by that—not because I do not like to be with him, but because it is overwhelmingly difficult to write anything that can compare to that presence. This is perhaps why I easily slip into writing theology in a way that avoids the direct conversation with Jesus we call prayer—not a good habit! I hope you fare better as you read this book, and as you and Christ work out together a real sense of who he is. So let's begin with desire, the desire that God arouses in you by speaking to you in Christ.

I like to think of myself as a reasonably stable individual who does certain things, thinks certain thoughts, and has a variety of feelings and desires— some of them good and helpful, and others distracting, not to say downright embarrassing. But fortunately, I think to myself, these acts and thoughts and feelings are all just passing ripples in the sea of selfhood that is really me; they are not "me" in any enduring sense. But then who exactly am I? Who or what is it, exactly, that constitutes "me"? On the one hand there is the physiological stuff that is "me": my genes and all the things they have determined about me, like my hair color (brown) and height (6' 2") and probably to a certain extent even my natural disposition or temperament. We might just call that my nature; it is *what* I am. But we know from studies of infant and childhood development that even twins who share virtually identical biological natures develop into different persons if they are raised in different environments. *What* I am is formed by circumstances into a particular *who*. In other words, my nature (what I am) and my person (who I am) are related but still distinct.

It may not be clear yet why this distinction between nature and person is worth bothering about, but at least you can see that it is fairly reasonable. After all, we often regard it as a great triumph of personal freedom and growth when someone is able to push beyond the ingrained patterns of his physiological *nature* to become a truly remarkable *person*—a child born blind, for example, who yet becomes a passionate and visionary musician. *Who* we become is not necessarily limited by *what* we are. Now the interesting question is: what or who arouses us from a life governed solely by the instinctual drives of need and survival, toward the blossoming of personal identity? What summoned us out of our childhood cribs to build sandcastles? What drew us from drooling on our blankets to fingerpainting to playing house to building housing developments to performing neurosurgery or writing theology? We might say that it is *desire* that "becomes" you, desire that leads to your becoming the person you are.

And here we need to be careful, because right away we are tempted to talk about these desires as though they were primarily our own, an aspect of ourselves that we possess, like our hair color. Let's say I have a desire for chocolate ice cream. This desire is mine. I own it, and I exist prior to it. But what I am suggesting is a bit more disturbing: that what you think of as "you" really comes *after* desire and as a *result* of desire. You have been brought into being by a desire that comes from beyond you and awakens you to yourself.

This awakening begins very early on. Your mother held a little cuddly bear and wiggled it around in front of you, showing you how delightful it was, and you, healthy little human animal that you were, immediately wanted it. Your mother *wanted* to arouse your desire for the bear by showing you how cute it was. She wanted to entice you into caring about something, and without realizing it, you were on your way to becoming you. And before you knew it, you were becoming a person all your own, someone shaped and imprinted and fully aroused by all the desires of the world around you, from the desires of your parents to those of your friends, your co-workers, and even your favorite television characters.

Maybe that is why so much of the great literature of childhood is about adventures and quests and arduous searches after unattainable prizes. These stories lead us by a strange and dangerous series of mysterious twists and turns, at the end of a long and perilous journey, into self-discovery. "Come, come, my dear," said the kindly old hedgehog in the story, as she wiped the grimy tears from the boy's face, "did you really believe that cruel woodcutter and his wife were your parents? Now then, child, just you look over the brow of this hill. Do you see those castle towers? . . . " Or one

day you find a queer old map hidden in a secret com-
partment of your grandfather's desk, or one night
you have a beautiful dream about a sacred chalice, a
holy grail. Or there is a sword to be pulled from a
stone, or a lost mother to be found...and we are off!
The story of our birth and coming into being appears
in these old fairy tales as the recovery of a secret identity, the reunion with someone able to tell us the truth
of who we are, someone whose recognition of us is the
deep desire of our hearts. But who is it really that tugs
so at our hearts, setting our hopes ablaze and our
spirits on fire? Who awakens in us such a yearning to
be, to be recognized, found, identified at long last as
the person we have finally become?

Christians believe that behind all our desiring and
working secretly within it is God's own desire, the
desire of the Father for the Son and the Son for the
Father, the desire we call God the Holy Spirit. That is
what awakens our own desire and into which we are
beckoned: behind all the childhood stories of mistaken
identities and long-lost parents who are finally found
stands the very One who has truly loved us from all
eternity and who knows every hair on our heads. It is
this yearning Holy Spirit who ignites our desire and
draws us into the life of Christ. Being filled with
Christ's burning desire to do the Father's will is the
truly great adventure—the one in which we must risk
all if we would find all, called and claimed at last as
God's own beloved child.

The nineteenth-century Anglican theologian and
priest John Neville Figgis captures this sense of being
drawn out of the self we think we are only to discover a more personal reality on the other side:

> You can never win any kind of peace or self-pos-
> session unless you have risked all to get it. Ask

yourself for one moment what have been your
feelings on the eve of some act involving
courage. . . . Have you not felt something like
this? "I cannot do this. This is too much for me.
I shall ruin myself if I take this risk. I cannot
take the leap. It is impossible. All me will be
gone if I do this, and I cling to myself." And then
supposing the spirit has conquered and you
have done this impossible thing, do not you find
afterwards that you possess yourself in a sense
that you never have before, that there is more of
you? . . . You know you are something different
from what you were before, and something
more.[1]

The survival instincts of our nature weigh us down
like gravity, telling us not to risk the very thing that
most enlivens us. For by giving freely of ourselves in
love we become the persons we long most to be: the
beloved ones of God.

∼ The Distortion of Desire

We are closer now to seeing how we can understand
Jesus by thinking about desire; even the earliest followers of Jesus began to recognize who Jesus is by
noticing how he restored their desire to wholeness. As
he transformed and healed and redirected their
desires, his disciples began to wonder who this person
could be. But the process of transformation is always
painful; it begins with a growing awareness, in the
light of Christ's loving, of how distorted our loving
has become. So before we turn directly to Jesus and
the Incarnation, it will be helpful to recall the story of
how this distortion comes about, and how it mangles
our capacity to love.

The world as God created it, the Bible hints, was meant to be a living, breathing sacrament of the giving life of the Trinity. Eden is the environment where every being could come to flourish in the fullness of its own identity by being freely for each other and with God. God brings the whole creation into being freely, for joy, to share in God's trinitarian life of mutual giving. God says, "It is not good that the man should be alone" (Genesis 2:18) and brings the other animals to *adam* to make their acquaintance and to receive names. Above all, God gives the man and woman to each other as signs of God's own life, the luminous image of God's freely loving existence. No being that existed was merely an object to be possessed; each was for itself and for all, tracing out in time and space that pattern of giving and receiving from which all things come. This is how we become fully persons, by sharing in God's life—a life in which the divine Persons simply *are*, by their mutual desire and delight.

Alas, as Genesis tells us, an immobilizing chill crept into this paradise. From the serpent's perspective, God is a miser, holding back the delicious fruit from Adam and Eve, and doing so out of a sense of rivalry. Perhaps, we think, this garden is just a hoax to keep *us* from getting the goods that God does not want to share, lest *we* should turn out to be just as good at being God, maybe even better! Maybe God should just get out of the way and let us grow up and be gods ourselves. Thus it happens—and happens over and over. The cuddly teddy bear your mother was delighted to put into your infant hands graduates into a desire for the car keys and the credit card, and beneath all that, into the fierce drive to be a "grown-up" yourself. Without anybody really noticing when it happened, your parents began to seem less like models, loving sources of all good, and more like painfully uncool obstacles to your being fully yourself.

This little pathology of family life is our initiation into a whole world of possessive rivalry. Instead of our world awakening us with a desire we joyously embrace, we continually ingest a tainted desire that makes us suspicious of everyone else on the assumption that they will either keep us from getting what we think we deserve or else manipulate us into giving it to them. The deity of this dominion of fear, not surprisingly, is the projection of our fallen sense of the other as dangerous rival. This all-powerful god we have begun to worship is punitive, jealous, full of wrath, ready to smack its creatures into oblivion for the slightest disobedience, thirsting for the sacrificial blood of atonement, and so righteous it will laugh our miserable attempts at holiness into eternal derision. No wonder so many people prefer only a passing acquaintance with this God seen through the eyes of the serpent.

Perhaps you think I am exaggerating? Many times I have visited people in hospital who greet me with a rueful sigh. "Well, Father," they ask me, "what did I do to deserve this?" There is an underlying paganism in most of us that seeps into our Christian faith and infects it with the fear that God will punish us if we are too happy, or afflict us with AIDS or cancer or ulcerative colitis if we step out of line, or require us to bargain in degrees of suffering for the health of our children.

This image of God as a vengeful, crushing rival to human flourishing is exactly what the prophets and teachers of Israel sought to overthrow. It is to set us free from this that Jesus died and rose again. How we might begin to think about this mystery of salvation is the stuff of the next chapter, but here we want simply to ask who Jesus is that he could liberate us from this kingdom of death. The witness of his followers is not that he saved them by his teaching or healing or way of life alone, but because of who he was in his teaching and healing and who it was they met in his dying and rising from death.

～ New Creation in Christ

What seems to have happened at Easter was that our tainted desire, distorted and infected by fear and antagonism, was subverted and undone. Jesus, the victim, far from remaining dead, comes looking for the very people who betrayed him the most deeply. Yet he comes not to haunt them or theaten them, but to *forgive* them. The testimony of the apostles is that out of Jesus' forgiving presence, alive and yet crucified, they were given new selves and made into a new creation. They were commissioned and sent out, filled with *his* desire—peaceful and true—through the Holy Spirit, and so made alive in a way that could no longer be enslaved to death.

In the resurrection the disciples were confronted so profoundly by Jesus as their forgiving and self-giving victim that the serpent's lie was utterly unmasked. Over and over the risen Lord says to us, "Do not be afraid." The disciples passed through the death of their poisoned desire and were raised up in Christ to the holy desire, Holy Spirit, who alone could make them free. Jesus seems to have literally inspired his friends—"He breathed on them and said to them, 'Receive the Holy Spirit'" (John 20:22)—not with a desire provoked by fear or nervous resistance, but with a desire of purely loving gratuity—"All that the Father has is mine" (John 16:15). The disciples died with Christ and lived with him, as St. Paul later wrote, and so they were restored to a relationship with God that was purified and healed of all the human taint of fear and anger.

So strong was their sense that they had been recreated that the disciples began to realize it could only come from something central to Jesus himself: his own identity. For Jesus brought them not a particular *message* about God but his own particular *relationship* with the Father, a relationship that made him the person he was and somehow recreated them as persons themselves. We can see something like this being described by St. Paul when he writes:

> God has sent the Spirit of his Son into our hearts, crying, "Abba! Father!" So you are no longer a slave but a child, and if a child then also an heir, through God [or, an heir of God through Christ]. (Galatians 4:6-7)

Interestingly, in the same passage Paul goes on to speak of how the Galatians had previously not known God and so "were enslaved to beings that by nature are not gods" (4:8). Paul is alarmed because his converts are so easily slipping back into that old demonic relationship with the divine that is marked by fear, the need to make special bargains and observe secret rituals in order to placate the powerful forces that threaten them. It is precisely this relationship ("I'll sacrifice so many goats for so many divine favors" or "If you'll just let the X-rays come back negative I promise I'll never...") from which Paul believes we have been freed by being drawn into Jesus' own relationship with the Father.

This relationship is inaugurated in us by the "Spirit of the Son," as Paul puts it, who pours out within us the trust and loving self-giving that identifies Jesus as the Son of God. By putting Jesus' own cry of desire to the Father, "Abba!", in our hearts, the Spirit makes us also adoptive heirs, the beloved of God in Christ the Beloved. Before this we were like the older brother in the parable of the prodigal son: hearing the party being thrown for the beloved "other" brother, we come sniffing around, assuming that once again both the rival brother and the Father are cheating us out of what we have earned for ourselves. We fail to realize that the life God wishes to shower on us, unlike any earthly relationship we have ever experienced, has no limits, so for the Father to give to someone else does not mean that we are left with any less.

It is this wounded, hostile relationship with God that Jesus is working to undo when we hear the father's gracious words to the older brother, "Son, you are always with me, and all that is mine is yours" (Luke 15:31). We have *always* been cherished by God, but we mistake this love for something that is fitful and arbitrary, a kind of foolish, addled indulgence that prefers some over others. The words "and all that is mine is yours" speak instead of that freely flowing divine life that God has always longed for us to share if only we can stop suspecting that it is all just a ruse.

What could break through our fear and suspicion? Nothing Jesus could say or do—otherwise the authorities would not have been provoked to murder him or the disciples to betray him. What began the new creation was precisely the disciples' encounter with the victim, the "other" whom they had gotten out of the way and abandoned. It was his forgiveness and healing of their broken lives that began the great work in them. The power of Christ's resurrection is the power that reveals the lie at the heart of our world, the lie that says our desire can only be fulfilled at the expense of another. This is the very heart of Christian faith. It seems to come not just from what Jesus said and did but from who he is. He embodied for the disciples a forgiving love they could only identify as God's own.

～ The Person Jesus Is

So far we have been thinking about how we become persons. I have been trying to describe how God's desire for us arouses our desire for God, and how this yearning pulls us beyond mere survival and into the freedom and relationships of true personhood. I have been suggesting that Jesus' followers experienced so profound a new creation of their personal lives that they began to recognize in him this divine power to create persons. Now we want to turn more directly to the questions that emerge when Jesus comes to be recognized in this way. What does it mean to say that Jesus is the Word or Son of God "incarnate"? How can we say that in Jesus we have met not merely a word about God, but God's own Word, existing humanly? That not only can human life be lived divinely, but that God can be human? I think we can find a fit among several important pieces of this puzzle: the way we come into our full personhood through desire, the way God exists as a desiring communion of divine Persons, and how the church, beginning at the resurrection, was given the Holy Spirit in order to participate in this personal communion of trinitarian love.

Can I prove all this? As far as "proving" things goes, I know some theologians believe we can prove that Christianity is true. I think that trying to "prove" Christianity by making it look like a generic religion actually does more harm than good. In some ways, the truthfulness of Christian faith has to be left in the tender hands of the Holy Spirit, who alone can convince us and lead us into all truth. My hunch is that the Spirit is far more likely to convince by moving us to pray and help at the night shelter and take some kids who have never seen a cow out to the country than by brooding over rational arguments. While I am not willing to try to prove the truth of the Incarnation, I will try to show that it is coherent: that the mystery we are being led to adore has a kind of logic we can grasp. So what follows is merely an attempt to show how thinking about Jesus in terms of the Incarnation makes sense; the *truth* of it is something I think we can only know in the end if we are willing to let the Holy Spirit work in us the mystery of Christ's dying and rising.

I have already said that Jesus is able to save us precisely because he embodies the relationship with the Father to which we need to be restored. So to understand who Jesus is, we need to ask how he could be said to "incarnate" this relationship. How is God present in the historical human being, Jesus of Nazareth? For most of Christian history, the answers to these questions have been spread across a wide range of positions.

At one extreme is the view that Jesus was just a very good man who told us something important about God. Whatever meaning Jesus has is not particularly related to who he was but to something he did or said: he showed us what God is like, or he gave us a new model of community that became a metaphor for understanding life. Because this insight is crucial, we can say that God was especially inspired or uniquely present in his life. But, at the end of the day, Jesus was simply human.

For those at the opposite extreme, Jesus is the divine Word pretending to be human. Jesus' humanity is insignificant, possibly even problematic, in the great divine work of salvation. In coming to redeem us, God the Son did reach out to us where we are and stoop down to our humanity, but basically he is simply divine. Both of these extremes are minimalist and they are easy positions to take: both avoid having to face the astonishing idea that God and humanity are *not* mutually exclusive after all.

It may be helpful to examine your own basic thoughts about Jesus in terms of this range of incarnational perspectives. Most of us tend to lean in one direction or the other, away from the seeming paradox of the center: Jesus is both fully human *and* the eternal Word of God. Has your underlying assumption been that Jesus is fundamentally a good man in whose life God was very deeply involved? Or have you tended to see Jesus in divine terms, perhaps as a wonderful but always unattainable ideal, someone unsullied by the tedious details and mean little hurts of our lives? Perhaps it would be interesting to think about the way you hear other people talk about Jesus; how would you "diagnose" their tendencies? In general, it is fair to say that Anglican theologians from Richard Hooker in the sixteenth century to Frederick Denison Maurice and Charles Gore in the nineteenth and William Temple and Michael Ramsey in the twentieth have all sought to avoid these two extremes and bring us into communion with the saving mystery of God's intimate presence in Christ.

～ Objections to the Incarnation

Perhaps the best way to understand this mystery better is to figure out together some responses to the usual objections to the doctrine of the Incarnation. By trying to understand the criticisms, see what resources the doctrine can muster in reply, and formulate something like an answer in our own terms, we may be able to practice a little theology together.

What are the criticisms of the Incarnation as a way of understanding Jesus? To begin with, since the time of the Enlightenment there has been a growing discomfort with the language of the Incarnation. Sometimes this is just a translation problem, as when people get themselves all worked up over the fact that when the fifth-century Council of Chalcedon used language of "one person" and "two natures" to talk about Jesus, it was not using those terms in the same way that we do. This difference is nothing to worry about, provided we have scholars who are historically informed enough to help us find the right language to express the same ideas.

Usually the complaint goes deeper: it is more than just a problem with the vocabulary of the church's teaching, but a question of whether its fundamental ideas make sense for today. In short, the argument runs, the incarnational conception may actually misrepresent the gospel because it centers all our attention on a myth of God coming to earth as a human being, which rational people today cannot hear without embarrassment. This critique prefers the intellectually plausible notion that it is not God who became incarnate but the *idea* of God's kingdom, which is coming into being in and through the community that Jesus created.

This view raises some important points by highlighting the social dimension at the heart of Christianity. Understanding Jesus in terms of the Incarnation, however, seems to have been precisely the engine that drove the early church's social awareness. Its relationships of forgiveness and love were understood to be the sign and test of its understanding of Jesus. The early Christians could tell whether they were truly entering into the mystery of Christ by how well they were managing to love one another, and in doing so they were forging the matrix on earth in which the trinitarian communion of loving self-giving and eternal joy could become available for all people, as John's gospel reports:

> Those who love me will keep my word, and my Father will love them, and we will come to them and make our home with them. . . . As the Father has loved me, so I have loved you; abide in my love. If you keep my commandments, you will abide in my love, just as I have kept my Father's commandments and abide in his love. I have said these things to you so that my joy may be in you, and that your joy may be complete. This is my commandment, that you love one another as I have loved you. (John 14:23, 15:9–12)

The coming kingdom of God flows from the joyful communion of the Trinity; it is foreshadowed in our world by the sacrament of the Christian community's life on earth together. And the mediator of that joy is Jesus, precisely because of his relationship with the Father. So, understanding Jesus in terms of the Incarnation (which means understanding something new about *God*) is not to ignore the gospel's social dimensions.

So let's look at another objection, the fear that the Incarnation is implausible today. My hunch is that many people, without thinking much about it, tend to assume that divine existence and human existence are mutually exclusive; by definition the Creator is not a creature and vice versa.[2] This objection was stated perhaps most notably in recent thought by the theologian John Hick, who wrote that "to say, without explanation, that the historical Jesus of Nazareth was also God is as devoid of meaning as to say that this circle drawn with a pencil on paper is also a square."[3]

Now in light of what we said in the chapter on creation, we might ask Hick a counter-question. What is he assuming about God in proposing an analogy between the relationship of the divine and human in Christ and the relationship of a circle and a square? Do we really want to say that the divine is related to the human the same way a circle is related to a square?

That is exactly the question! Circles and squares inhabit the same space; they are items in the same universe. But the mystery of creation is all about the fact that God is not one *item* in the universe at all, not even the biggest and most powerful item. God is not a thing—like a sheep or an asteroid or a television commercial—that we would have to rule out if we wanted to make sure that we were dealing with just an ordinary human being, since it is not possible to be a human being and an asteroid at the same time. But since God is the sheer Living that makes it possible for there to be anything at all, God is never one of the things over against which there is one particular thing we call human.

True, it makes no sense to say that a circle is also a square. But to say that a human being called Jesus is also divine is *not* the same thing. To say that this human being is also divine is more like saying that when I hug my children, it is also Love who hugs them. Please note that this does not mean that Love is hugging my children *instead* of me, or that I am less myself in hugging my children because I love them. On the contrary, my freedom and desire to hug my children come about because of this Love. This Love and I are not mutually exclusive: just because Love is at work in the act of my children being hugged, it still is me hugging them! In fact, Love is the source of my act. It empowers my act and helps me to fulfill myself as a parent, and so while it is really and truly I who am doing the hugging, we could reasonably say that it is also Love hugging my children—Love embodied in me.

God's relationship to our human being is more like its source and power, not another item alongside the human that might from time to time butt in and take over. When I hug my children, it is not an asteroid or a postage stamp that is hugging them. So to say that this human being is also *divine* is not the same as saying that this human being is also a horse, or that this circle is also a square.

But besides this merely logical confusion over the relationship between divine existence and human existence, there is another, deeper confusion. It stems from a failure to take advantage of a crucial distinction arrived at in early Christianity and one I introduced earlier in this chapter: the distinction between nature, or *what* we are, and person, or *who* we are. While this distinction became crucial in the church's understanding of the Trinity (three divine Persons as one divine Nature), it also has an extremely valuable role to play in thinking about the mystery of the Incarnation. For the distinction allows us to say that the union of divine and human in Jesus does *not* happen in terms of nature. Why is this important? Because a union of "natures" raises exactly the same question from which we were trying to extricate ourselves just now.

Christians have always resisted the idea that Jesus is both God and human because he is some kind of mixture of the two natures. Whenever people have taken this path they always have gone awry because they cannot quite figure out how to whip together the divine "stuff" and the human "stuff," and they always end up with some concoction that does not do justice to either. When they are totally mingled, we may get a curious, amphibious sort of Jesus who may have a human body but not a human soul or mind; the divine nature, which is supposedly suited to the soul and mind business, simply takes over that part of Jesus' human nature. Or we may get a divine nature that has suffered catastrophic memory loss and is slumming around in human suffering because it has given up its divine prerogatives. When they are kept separate, however, with the two natures simply yoked together in some way, then we get Jesus One and Jesus Two, like a game of me and my shadow, where the perfectly ordinary and wonderfully blessed Jesus has a divine counterpart called "the Son," who comes along for the ride but hovers safely above the human fray.

It was exactly to rule out these kinds of parlor games that the Council of Chalcedon included the following words in their definition of healthy talk about Jesus:

> One and the same Christ, Son, Lord, Only-begotten, recognized in two natures, *without confusion, without change, without division, without separation;* the distinction of natures being in no way annulled by the union, but rather the characteristics of each nature being preserved and coming together to form one person and subsistence, not as parted or separated into two persons, but one and the same Son and Only-begotten God the Word, Lord Jesus Christ. (BCP 864; *my emphasis*)

Notice how the set of four qualifiers that I have highlighted pairs off to avoid the two problems I was just mentioning? "Without confusion, without change" rules out any mixture of the natures in which we end up with something neither fish nor fowl. "Without

division, without separation" rules out the good-
fences-make-good-neighbors approach to understanding Jesus, in which the divine and the human
natures are never quite allowed to share fully in each
other's existence. What the Chalcedonian Definition
points to instead is a union and unity of Christ that
takes place in terms of *person*, in terms of *who* Jesus is.

Our word "person" comes from the Greek word
prosopon, derived from *pros*, meaning "to" or "toward"
and *ops*, *opos* (as in "optics"), meaning "look" or "face."
So to be a "person" or *pros-opon* in this original trinitarian sense means to be one "facing toward" another.
What marks each of the three "facing toward," or
divine Persons, is the particular pattern of relationship
they have to one another. That is *who* they are. There
is the personal pattern of Fatherhood, of giving more
and more and holding nothing back. There is the personal pattern of Sonship, of receiving more and more
and eternally "speaking" that giving love. There is the
personal pattern of Spirithood, of being the love who
draws One ever toward Another. And, Christians
believe, it is the *second* of these patterns, the personal
pattern of loving we call Word, or Son, that is Jesus'
identity.

Now immediately you might say, but does that
mean that Jesus is not a real human person, since we
have just said he is a divine Person? The answer is no,
it does not. Christians have never said Jesus did not
have his own psychology, character traits, and the
uniquely *personal* inclinations that make people who
they are. What Christians have always said is that the
completely and like-us-in-every-way *human being*
Jesus, who preached, taught, wept, prayed, hungered,
slept, and doubtless cleaned his teeth and cut his fin-
gers, was living out the personal pattern of loving we
call Son. The very same pattern of personhood that

distinguishes Jesus from the apostle Peter, from you or me, is the very same personhood that distinguishes God the Word from God the Father or God the Holy Spirit.

Consider an analogy. In most families with a number of children, every child develops a particular role that becomes part of them—this one is the peacemaker, that one the joker, and so on. Similarly, in the "family life" of a parish, you can see some of the same roles coming out and marking individuals as the particular persons they are. Often we are made aware of this in uncomfortable ways, such as when someone in a vestry meeting reacts violently to a proposal to change the narthex wall color. But take a slightly more subtle example: the same person who always picked up her little brother when he fell off his bike years ago brings to the parish family her habits of patience for the obviously vulnerable and reserve for the seemingly self-confident. The same pattern of personhood is there, first at home and now at church, but the circumstances under which that personal presence comes to be lived out, *incarnated*, may be somewhat different—caring for scraped knees in one case and running the soup kitchen in another. In an analogous way, I am suggesting, the eternal Word's pattern of filial love and trusting relationship with the Father in their Spirit is the very same pattern of personal presence that expresses itself, becomes incarnate, in the circumstances of *our* world as Jesus of Nazareth.

The fact that Jesus is a divine Person does not mean that he is not human, for the person he is tells us *who* and not *what* he is. The brutal truth is that we have managed to make a world in which being human in this particular way—living according to the loving relationship of the Son to the Father—gets us crucified. It means identifying ourselves with the cross. But as we know well enough, being marked with the cross does not take away our humanity. It does, however, begin to open before us a new way of being *who we are*, a new way of being human that has been baptized into the way of God's own Beloved, a way of being a new person in Christ.

One very helpful approach for getting at the significance of this distinction between nature and person is an insight arrived at by two Anglicans of the nineteenth and twentieth centuries, John Henry Newman and Austin Farrer. Too often, Newman argues, we simply look at the question of trying to understand the Incarnation from the outside, as though it were an arcane puzzle. But when we are drawn to consider the meaning of the Incarnation from *within*—from Jesus' point of view—we see over and over that what he longs to fulfill is not some divine tendency, but his actual mission of loving obedience to the Father, that particular pattern of relationship that identifies him as who he is.

If we simply scratch our heads over how divine nature could mysteriously become human stuff, then it seems as though we must be talking about a change in the nature of God or of human being. But, says Newman, if we allow our thinking to be attuned to that pattern of activity we call "sonship," then we might begin to sense how "to continue the idea of a Son into that of a servant, though the descent was infinite." That is, we could conceive of how the eternal Son would be carrying out his *personal role* of loving expression of the Father by enacting that role, in our time and space, as a suffering human servant.[4]

We can see the same idea at work in Austin Farrer, preaching in the same city as Newman just over a century later. Because he states the fundamental point so very well, I am going to quote a large bit, but do notice especially what he is saying at the end of the passage.

> We cannot understand Jesus as simply the God-who-was-man. We have left out an essential factor, the sonship. Jesus is not simply God manifest as man; he is the divine Son coming into manhood. What was expressed in human terms here below was not bare deity; it was the divine sonship. God cannot live an identically godlike life in eternity and in a human story. But the divine Son can make an identical response to his Father, whether in the love of the blessed Trinity or in the fulfilment of an earthly ministry. All the conditions of action are different on the two levels; the filial response is one. Above, the appropriate response is a co-operation in sovereignty and an interchange of eternal joys. Then the Son gives back to the Father all that the Father is. Below, in the incarnate life, the appropriate response is an obedience to inspiration, a waiting for direction, an acceptance of suffering, a rectitude of choice, a resistance to temptation, a willingness to die. For such things are the stuff of our existence; and it was in this very stuff that Christ worked out the theme of heavenly sonship, proving himself on earth the very thing he was in heaven... a continuous perfect act of filial love.[5]

"Your will be done on earth as in heaven," we pray, in the one prayer Jesus taught us. This vision of the Father's will becoming real on earth as it is in heaven was so much on Jesus' heart because it was the very core and center of his identity. He was and is the one who *is* who he is by living to do the Father's will. He is the eternal Speaking of God's loving and giving life, not only in heaven's language but also in the lame and disjointed speech that we have made of human existence. We could even say that the divine Word of God's rescuing love is most completely expressed by *being human*, by finding us exactly where we are, and by entering ever more deeply into the depths of our life. For it is this searching us out and carrying us home, this readiness to share completely in our most hopeless forms of lostness, that speaks most eloquently of the infinitely giving love of God. It is to this rescuing action of the Word, concentrated in the dying and rising of Jesus, that we turn next.

Chapter Six

The Glory of Humanity

The Mystery of Salvation

> He felt a loneliness he'd not known since child-
> hood and he felt wholly alien to the world
> although he loved it still.
>
> —*Cormac McCarthy*

So Cormac McCarthy describes the young hero of his novel *All the Pretty Horses*. John Grady Cole is becoming a man, embarking on a journey in which independence would come only at the price of loneliness, the aching of love, and violence. McCarthy's novel, so spare and yet so richly evocative of all the great and dangerous myths of American life, is a potent vision of the isolation and antagonism that being an adult seems to entail.

God, Christians believe, saves us in the midst of all the chaos and clamor of this world we have made, where love and beauty are rare and costly things. John Grady Cole travels through this strange econo-my of life. He reflects on the painful and seemingly inexplicable exchanges between good and evil, love and hate, that seem to be required by our world:

> He thought that in the beauty of the world were hid a secret. He thought the world's heart beat at some terrible cost and that the world's pain and its beauty moved in a relationship of diverging equity and that in this headlong deficit the blood of multitudes might ultimately be exacted for the vision of a single flower.[1]

It is as though passage into adulthood has to include a grievous initiation into the terrible cost of life. The national news has been filled repeatedly in recent years with stories and images of deadly violence by children against children in schools around the country. Some of the young people who committed the violence were involved in satanism, and there are rumors of their exposure to obscene, violent music, of embittered jealousy and hateful retribution. It seems that these children, our children, have been brutally exposed to the "knowledge of good and evil" so early that they can no longer find a life, an identity, for themselves apart from death—as though life is only defined for them in terms of death.

This is the culture, the way of the world, in which Jesus comes to find us—and we know that this *is* where he finds us, for on the cross we see what the world does to him. The question this chapter explores is how he *delivers* us in this world and creates in our new lives the beginning of a *new* world. Theology calls this question the mystery of salvation.

∿ The Nature of Evil

We might say that the painful suffering of our world is simply the way things naturally are, that at the heart of things lies an original violence, and when left to our own devices we tend to destroy others in order to reap the spoils ourselves. In some ways this perspective undergirds much of our own modern western view of the world. It was articulated most succinctly by the English political philosopher Thomas Hobbes, who in the seventeenth century called human life in its natural state "solitary, poor, nasty, brutish, and short." Hobbes argued that civil society needs to take its bearings from this original fact of violence rather than from any optimism about the goals and ends of human life. Later theories about evolution took this image of violence one step further; Social Darwinists saw the process by which you and I have come to be as a long and bloody struggle for the "survival of the fittest," where the price of growth and flourishing is the obliteration of the weak by the strong—weak genes by strong genes, inferior species by superior species, feeble economies by robust economies. As John Grady Cole sensed, there is only a limited amount of life to be had, and if I am going to have *my* share then yours must be crushed and poured out to me.

In the last chapter I suggested that Jesus' first followers found themselves confronted by a very different kind of "economy," an economy of overflowing life in which the last become first, the meek inherit the earth, and the dead are made to live with the sheer aliveness of God. The power of Jesus' resurrection exposes the economy of death as a vicious lie, a mesmerizing illusion. The resurrection confronts us with the possibility that without even realizing it, humankind has been so blinded by envy, fear, and violence that the true life of God has become unimaginable. I am not sure we can even realize how things *are* with us until we have been forced to see the impact of our world on Jesus and vice versa.

The cross is this point of impact. In the letter to the Hebrews, the writer senses that by entering completely into the situation of God's children, Jesus is able to destroy the lie about death's ultimacy and so pry us loose from its grip:

> Since, therefore, the children share flesh and blood, he himself [Christ] shared the same things, so that through death he might destroy the one who has the power of death, that is, the devil, and free those who all their lives were held in slavery by the fear of death. (Hebrews 2:14–15)

It is significant that these themes of fear, death, and the power of an unrecognized lie are woven together more than once in the New Testament (see John 8:39–59 and Romans 8:15–17); indeed, I think their confluence takes us right to the edge of the void, to the power of nothingness and chaos.

Such evil has no life or energy of its own, but being parasitic and hidden, it only shows itself through the benign face of its hosts. Like any nightmare, evil can only gain a foothold in reality if we are so afraid of it that we allow it to become the basis for our own lives. The one thing that might threaten and unmask this lie is someone who is not only free of it as an individual but is able to organize a whole community with the energy and power to expose it. Jesus and the community forming around him posed a threat to the way of death and so forced it out nakedly into the open.

The author of Revelation describes in a vision one such moment of uncovering, of apocalypse, as the way of Jesus began to confront the political and social forces of the world:

> A great portent appeared in heaven: a woman
> clothed with the sun, with the moon under her
> feet, and on her head a crown of twelve stars.
> She was pregnant and was crying out in birth-
> pangs, in the agony of giving birth. . . . Then the
> dragon stood before the woman who was about
> to bear a child, so that he might devour her
> child as soon as it was born. . . . Then the drag-
> on was angry with the woman, and went off to
> make war on the rest of her children, those who
> keep the commandments of God and hold the
> testimony of Jesus. (Revelation 12:1-2, 4, 17)

Notice how the subtle insinuating serpent of Genesis 3—who only *hints* that perhaps God is our rival, someone to fear and resent—has by the book of Revelation been exposed as a raging dragon. The way of Jesus, coming to life through the humility and compassion of Jesus' community, forces the way of death to reveal itself as a pattern of fear, rejection, and a violence that would possess and corrupt all human structures.

Perhaps what I am writing seems farfetched to you. After all, neither you nor I are mass-killers with a secret "enemies list," but our ability to be well-behaved people most of the time would be mortally foolish grounds on which to conclude that the world is in general a good place. We have, I suspect, been tricked by our culture to think of sin only in individual terms: we are oblivious to how easily "niceness" comes to us because we have surrounded ourselves with defenses that very nicely strangle the life out of anyone or anything that gets in our way. To verify that all is not as it should be, just look at the questions put to us at the time of baptism:

Do you renounce Satan and all the spiritual
forces of wickedness that rebel against God?
I renounce them.
Do you renounce the evil powers of this world
which corrupt and destroy the creatures of
God?
I renounce them.
Do you renounce all sinful desires that draw
you from the love of God?
I renounce them. (BCP 302)

That is a serious series of renunciations. It describes
the world not as a pleasant place, but as the scene of
malignant rebellion against God, a power so seductive
that it is capable of drawing us into complicity. Even
if we take the language of the baptismal rite as a
metaphor, it still points to destruction and alienation
on a cosmic scale—a web of antagonism toward God
and God's creatures into which we can be snared as
individuals. The danger is that the system is so all-
enveloping that we only catch a glimpse of it from
time to time, and so never notice how our whole lives
may unknowingly be encircled by its net. Its cleverest
ploy is not simply to hide the reality of evil, for that
is hard to do, but to keep us so busy fretting over our
own personal and "private" sins that we assume the
sin of the world is just an extension of our own bad
habits. Thus even an awareness of sin can be used by
sin to immure us more deeply in sin.

Sometimes when I realize I have hurt someone I
love and I go to apologize, I am overwhelmed by the
unexpected depth of the other person's forgiveness. It
shocks me into realizing how strained our relationship has been. I think that the overwhelming presence
of the crucified and risen Jesus, and the stunning
power of forgiveness he poured out, began to open the

disciples' eyes in just this way. They realized with a kind of shock the vast extent of their enslavement to death. For just imagine how the official condemnation and execution of Jesus must have seemed to his followers. James Alison has acutely analyzed what the effect of the judicial lynching of Jesus was likely to be on his followers:

> Now it's possible that Jesus' disciples may have been pretty cynical with relation to the authorities, religious and others, in Israel. However, it's extremely unlikely that, when he died, they didn't come to accept something of those authorities' point of view about Jesus. Death is final and puts to an end the voice of the dissident, making those who killed him or her seem decent and reasonable people: after all, one's got to carry on living with them. The disciples on their way to Emmaus were sunk in the grief of those for whom Jesus' death was the triumph of the point of view of his persecutors. This viewpoint worked like this: this Jesus was a sinner, and in killing him, God's will was being done, since he had broken God's law. His death included hanging on a tree, which meant, according to Deuteronomy (Deut. 21:23; cf. Gal. 3:13), that he died under the curse of God.[2]

So the grip of death's dominion would seem to have been legitimated by Jesus' execution: it turned out that he had simply been wrong all along.

But what if the person you condemn to death is raised from the dead with healing and forgiveness for you? Then

> the whole system of thought which had led to his execution is called into question. In the first

place it means that Jesus had been right in the testimony which he had given about God: God is indeed the one whom Jesus had described and that means that God is not like Jesus' adversaries had claimed him to be. So the reasons given for doing away with Jesus were not reasons, but part of a sinful human mechanism for getting rid of people, which has nothing to do with God.[3]

In other words, the disciples begin to see not only how ensnared they were by fear and death, but how tainted even their idea of God had become. For by raising Jesus from the dead, God showed that Jesus' death had nothing to do with God. It was not God's handiwork to torture the Beloved or abandon and betray him.

～ Sin and the Fall

What do we need to be saved from? I have been suggesting that we cannot begin to recognize and understand "sin" just by looking around for something unpleasant, because sin has become so much a regular part of our lives that we are unable to see it for what it is. Worse than that, as religious people we tend to allow this distortion to infest even our sense of relationship with God. It lies hidden in our vision of God's justice, wrath, and jealous love, breeding in us an antagonism toward God through the very religious practices by which we obey and serve. It murmurs to us of how mighty and powerful is our God, and if we just do our part then God will reward us. It insinuates that the suffering and victimization we see going on around us is really nothing to worry about; it is simply God's just judgment and condemnation of the wicked and all those other people who are not as we are.

So far, we have been trying to approach the mystery of salvation by assuming that we do not really know *what* needs saving, or how. When theologians have spoken in the past of salvation from "original sin," they have pointed to many likely suspects for what seems to lie at the root of human disintegration: idolatry, pride, self-hatred, fear, and many other evils. One thing these all have in common is a hideous distortion in the relationship between the world and God. It is as if humanity, by refusing over and over to risk a freely given love of others, both human and divine, has constantly slipped into violent and mortal self-preservation. This fearful isolation of ourselves from each other can take the form of manipulation or oppression, but it can also lead to hopeless submission and acquiescence in the violence projected onto ourselves and others.

In the previous chapter on the Incarnation I suggested that the desire aroused in us by others, and through them by God, makes us become the persons we are called to be. But suppose that this desire became infected with mistrust and antagonism? Then the possibility of us each becoming healthy, loving persons would be warped and stunted; we would not risk the love of others that alone can draw us into real personhood. Instead, we would become caricatures of ourselves, enslaved to death, engaged in a constant search for mastery over others or else crushed by despair into some kind of hopeless abnegation of ourselves. Something very much like this is at work in the conflicts of our world, between races, between ethnic and religious communities, between social classes, between the sexes, between family members, and between dimensions of the human self.

How does it happen? One way of understanding it is to start with the love of God that first called us into being. This gift of existence always takes a very special form—it is an invitation into fellowship with God. Surely the Genesis story of God creating humankind in a wonderful garden, surrounded on every hand by divine bounty and splendor, is about the best picture one could have of this gift of existence as invitation to loving fellowship. In the words of the eucharistic prayer, God gives "the whole world into our care, so that, in obedience to you, our Creator, we might rule and serve all your creatures" (BCP 373) and everything exists as a means of communion with its Giver. God does not simply give us things to possess but gives the world "into our care" as a means of fellowship with the rest of creation and with God the Creator, who gives us a role in the divine creativity: "The LORD God took the man and put him in the garden of Eden to till it and keep it" (Genesis 2:15). This giving, receiving, caring, and nourishing is crystallized in the gift of food, where the gift of existence is communion and fellowship with the giver: we take the creation up into our very life as nourishment, by God's gift. The whole creation is a sign of God's loving presence.

Suppose you invite me to your house for a dinner party. I arrive and later, as we enjoy one another's company, the appetizers and meal itself become a wonderfully delicious sign, a sacrament, of our fellowship, a means of being *with* each other in mutual delight. But what if instead I arrive at your house and grab up your food and drink, gulping it down in a corner by myself, and slip back out? In that case, the gift of your hospitality can no longer be a basis for fellowship because I have debased it. It is important to remember that by inviting me, you are implicitly allowing me this option. My communion with you must be freely and joyfully desired, a celebration of fellowship with you.

In Paradise, God offered the whole creation as a continual sign of the gift of our existence, its basis and nourishment. We are created by this invitation to communion. So if we accept the whole creation and each other as a means of loving communion with God, and give *ourselves* away in love as a sign of God's love for others, then we are being drawn into fullness of life. But if we begin to have doubts, and begin to suspect that we would be better off grabbing these things for ourselves *apart* from fellowship with God, then we have a different kettle of fish.

For then we are desiring not the communion with God and each other that alone makes us into true persons, but mere biological survival. We try to "complete" ourselves not by taking what God longs to *give* us, but by what we can manage to devour on our own. Consider how an infant is drawn into relationship with others through cuddling and nurturing and feeding, becoming herself by means of the loving cooing and chattering that go on at every feeding time. But what if she were to be separated from the loving caregiver and fed with milk and cereal left impersonally in a dish in a corner of the crib? Pretty soon you would have a little creature whose personhood was withering away until finally all that was left was simply the biological need to survive.

Such a picture is painted for us by the story of the tempting serpent, who searched for some corner that could be infected with suspicion, doubt, mistrust, and fear of God. Finally we begin to *act* out of that mistrust, to act in a way that seeks to possess and control life for ourselves instead of seeing it as an infinite gift of relationship with God. The Genesis story goes on to hint at the new conditions of this fallen, counterfeit version of life: shame and suspicion in the presence of one another, fear and finger-pointing, the alienation of creation from itself.

What Jesus' resurrection shows us is that this spiral away from true life has woven itself into the very fabric of our world. We usually think of this fear in private terms, but the violence and submission that infect the world is legitimized by countless social structures, cultural practices, and economic imperatives that bring far more havoc and death than any individual alone could muster. The whole creation, given into humankind's care in order to become a means of communion with God, has itself been "subjected to futility" and in "bondage to decay" (Romans 8:20, 21). The world is no longer our communion with God; it is a disposable object.

∿ Ways to Think about Salvation
We have been trying to see what is wrong with the world by seeing what Jesus' death and resurrection tell us about it. As Christians continue to ponder the mystery of Jesus' saving work, a number of different images and models for thinking about salvation have evolved. The reality is so wonderful that no single way of thinking about salvation can ever be adequate, but at least we can notice how the language of these different models shapes our thinking about what God is doing.

The most fundamental question is this: Did Jesus really have to die to save us, and does his rising from the dead also play a role? The first thing we can say is that if, as I suggested above, Jesus' resurrection was God's loving vindication of Jesus, then the authorities who claimed that his death was according to God's law were mistaken. It is not God who condemned Jesus to the cross, but humankind.

And how did God respond to the evil that was unmasked in the world's rejection of Jesus? God's infinite loving was not pulled into the distorted language of our violence, nor did God answer our rejection of Jesus with counter-violence and destruction. No, in the resurrection God mercifully drew our violent speech into deeper, more peaceful speech, making our "no" into an infinite "yes." The resurrection of Jesus is not simply a counterpart to his death, or an equal and opposite reaction to our violence, but the embracing and healing of our violence by swallowing it up in God's loving. Jesus' whole life, with all its relationships, its wounds, and its dying—it is all given back to him glorified, infinitely living, vivacious, transparent to the Speaking of God in it all.

So even the last enemy, death, is defanged. The resurrection does not just reverse Jesus' death, wiping it out as though it had never occurred, for that would mean death really is something awful and terrifying, something to be hidden away and split off. Then death would simply be suppressed like a dark psychological urge; it could still enthrall us into acting out of fear. The resurrection of Jesus shows that even death itself can be befriended, loved back into its proper role in God's loving plan, rewoven into the fabric of creation as the means of giving ourselves most completely to God.

So Jesus' death is *not* something that God has directly brought about; neither is it accidental, just the unfortunate if inevitable result of being human in a vicious world. On the contrary, his death "allows" Jesus the opportunity to be utterly and perfectly human, entrusting himself completely into our hands and into the hands of his Father. His death, in other words, allows him to show us the humanity that lies hidden, dormant, or defeated in most of us—the humanity we were created to enjoy, forgiving and compassionate. It allows Jesus to take the tragic drama we have made of the world and restore to it its true end and goal. Jesus transforms the last and greatest act of human life, our dying, into a complete bestowal of ourselves into the hands of God.

The second major question in thinking about salvation is this: To whom is Jesus' saving work directed? There are roughly three ways of answering this question. One idea, found among many early Christians, is that Jesus' work is directed against the power of *evil*. Throughout his ministry, and on the cross, Jesus unmasks the role evil plays in our world. He suffers the effects of this evil without allowing it to infect him, and so destroys it. A second view, associated in some of its forms with the early twelfth-century theologian Peter Abelard, is that Jesus' work is primarily directed at *humanity*. Jesus gives the human race a new example of loving self-giving, and moves us to a new level of compassion and repentance, leading to a holy way of life. A third perspective, linked in some forms with St. Anselm, writing a generation before Abelard, is that Jesus' work is directed toward *God*. By his suffering and death Jesus pays back to God the debt of obedience humanity owes. In some later versions of this perspective, often associated with John Calvin in the sixteenth century, Jesus is seen in his suffering and death as bearing the infinite wrath of God against sin.

What we said earlier about what is happening in Jesus' death and resurrection can help us as we think about these different perspectives. Right away I would want to rule out the idea that what Jesus does in saving us is *solely* directed at his fellow human beings. To say that all Jesus gives us is a poignant example to help us act more decently in our own lives is rational and unmythological, but dangerously weak-kneed. Are all the things that separate you from God's love simply problems that can be solved by giving you a better example of how to act, as if that would correct things? Is the God of scripture more interested in setting a good example than in liberating people from slavery? On the other hand, this perspective reminds us that Jesus *does* show us the truth of our humanity and forge a community in which, by grace, our own humanity may be restored to life. And certainly our communion in Christ's sufferings may lead to the transformation of our own.

I think we can also rule out the idea that Jesus' death is solely a transaction between him and Satan. The cross is not a clever ploy in which Jesus tricks the devil into "biting off more than he could chew" in trying to kill the Son of God disguised as an ordinary man, for Jesus did not operate by trickery. Nor is his death on the cross a ransom *owed* to the devil as the price for releasing humanity from slavery to death— would God give ownership rights over any beloved creatures to some alien power, especially evil? On the other hand, Jesus' loving self-giving does expose the evil that dominates so much of life. And his acceptance of his death, handing himself over to the Father, denies death a final say over any human being.

With the third perspective, I think we must rule out any idea that Jesus was tortured to death by God the Father as a just retribution for humankind's offenses against divine justice, or as a necessary penalty to satisfy the divine honor. Yet these ideas are very difficult either to let go of or to live with, and so they all too often provoke a numbed silence in many faithful Christians. It is certainly true that the Bible has a lot to say about the wrath and vengeance and justice of God, but there are some points we can raise that weigh heavily against this idea of Jesus suffering God's retribution for our sin.

First, there is the fact that this particular (and powerful) reading of the Bible is alien to the entire eastern half of the church and so has a hard time claiming any universal agreement. A prominent Eastern Orthodox theologian, Christos Yannaras, has criticized this theory of Jesus suffering to appease God's wrath as a grotesque distortion not only of the truth about God, but also the truth about human sin:

> The changes which this theory occasioned in the faith of the Church are literally incalculable. It changed the truth of God by subordinating the freedom of his love to the relentless necessity of an egocentric and savage justice which demand-ed sadistic satisfaction. The God of the Church, from being a Father and "passionate lover" of mankind, was transformed into an implacable judge and menacing avenger whose justice rejoices . . . when it sees the sinners who are being tormented in hell.[4]

Yannaras argues that both judicial traditions from the Roman empire and the perspectives of western indi-vidualism have come together in this theory to distort and reinterpret God's loving self-giving to the *whole world* into a legal and penal transaction for the allevi-ation of individual guilt. He also suggests that it is no wonder, given the dominance of this theory in the west since the time of the Reformation, that so many westerners have rebelled against such a punitive idea and ended up as atheists.

A second critique of this perspective comes from contemporary feminist theology, which has universally criticized this theory of punitive suffering. As Roman Catholic theologian Elizabeth Johnson notes:

> Feminist theology repudiates an interpretation of the death of Jesus as required by God in repayment for sin. Such a view today is virtually inseparable from an underlying image of God as an angry, bloodthirsty, violent and sadistic father, reflecting the very worst of male behavior. Rather, Jesus' death was an act of violence brought about by threatened human men, as sin, and therefore against the will of a gracious God. . . . What comes clear in the event, however, is not Jesus' necessary passive victimization divinely decreed as a penalty for sin, but rather a dialectic of disaster and powerful human love through which the gracious God of Jesus enters into solidarity with all those who suffer and are lost.[5]

Jesus' suffering, in other words, far from being the price God demands in order to love us once more, is in fact the wounded heart of God's own solidarity with us in our separation from God. Jesus on the cross is God finding us in all our brokenness and isolation and coming to be with us in an irreversible and liberating way.

There is still a third reason for rejecting this interpretation of Jesus' crucifixion. Throughout this chapter and its predecessor we have seen how the resurrection overturned the disciples' understanding of themselves and of God. It led to a growing, peaceful enlargement of their minds and hearts by the "mind of Christ" (1 Corinthians 2:16; Philippians 2:5), as they came to share more and more in Jesus' own understanding of the Father. And a central part of that understanding is that the god of "Yes, but. . . ," the god whose love comes only at a painful price, is a dangerous lie about God. We can see signs in the early Christian community of how this new gift of the mind of Christ, of Christ's absolute trust in the loving *Abba*, took shape in believers' own hearts. Consider an important passage from John, where Jesus clearly teaches that his own death and the violence against the disciples is a sign of humanity's false relationship to God:

> If the world hates you, be aware that it hated me before it hated you. If you belonged to the world, the world would love you as its own. . . . But *they will do all these things to you on account of my name, because they do not know him who sent me.* If I had not come and spoken to them, they would not have sin; but now they have no excuse for their sin. Whoever hates me hates my Father also. If I had not done among them the works that no one else did, they would not have sin. But *now they have seen and hated both me and my Father.* . . . When the Advocate comes, whom I will send to you from the Father, the Spirit of truth who comes from the Father, he will testify on my behalf. . . . An hour is coming when *those who kill you will think that by doing so they are offering worship to God.* And they *will do this because they have not known the Father or me.* (John 15:18-19, 21-24, 26; 16:2-3; *my emphasis*)

This striking passage highlights three crucial points. First, Jesus' teaching of the true God's coming kingdom provokes evil into showing itself for what it is, a violent rejection of God and an aversion to true life. Because of what Jesus says and does, humankind "has sin": it clearly *sees* the truth of God, but just as clearly reveals its sinful *rejection* of God.

Second, the killing of Jesus and attacks on the disciples are not something God has ordained to "get back" at creation, but the reaction of fallen humanity to God's self-revelation in Jesus. All violence is unmasked as a horrible projection of human fear and anger onto God, a demon god whom humanity thinks it is worshiping by killing Jesus and the disciples ("those who kill you will think that by doing so they are offering worship to God"). Third, Jesus' own relationship with the Father as loving and trustworthy will be vindicated after his death by a living and life-giving Spirit, which will inhabit and cleanse and heal the disciples' own hearts and minds, bearing witness to the truth of the Father's love for Christ and leading the disciples into that love themselves.

Perhaps we should pause here to address what may be a lingering question. Doesn't God punish sin? Isn't God angry at what is evil, and insofar as Jesus is bearing the sins of the world, then wouldn't God's punishment fall on him? These questions truly merit a book in themselves, but I think we have to interpret biblical language about God's wrath and Jesus' suffering of God's wrath in the terms I have spoken of above. We have to allow the whole pattern of Jesus' life, death, resurrection, ascension, and sending of the Spirit to be the rule that interprets all of scripture. In other words, I think our experience of *human* justice, anger, and punishment has distorted our thinking about God by focusing our minds upon what loathsome and disgusting creatures we are that God should need to punish us so much. Ironically, this focus obscures our loving rescue by God in Christ that Christ's death has accomplished.

I believe that Jesus' self-surrender and resurrection have begun to dismantle irreversibly our idolatry of power and anger, liberating us into that true power that, as St. Paul saw, looks to the world like foolishness and weakness. I believe that as a result of the spreading and deepening impact of the resurrection, we can see a progressive reinterpretation of all this imagery within the New Testament itself. By the time of John's gospel (usually considered the last of the gospels to be finished), we have a complete reversal. Far from demanding a violent pay-off for all our sinning, God tenders to us a self-offering as a way of reestablishing communion with us, freeing us from subjection to evil and so restoring us to life and fellowship. See if this view does not bring to the surface what we often overlook in this famous passage:

> For God so loved the world that he gave his only Son, so that everyone who believes in him may not perish but may have eternal life. Indeed, God did not send the Son into the world to condemn the world, but in order that the world might be saved through him.... And this is the judgment, that the light has come into the world, and people loved darkness rather than light. (John 3:16-17, 19)

Judgment, wrath, and condemnation are not something that God pours out. They are what we experience when we refuse to repent and return to the Lord: they are the experience of being cut off from God and enslaved to idols of our own making. Sometimes when I have acted badly, I feel so frustrated with myself that I just seethe in my own anger, refusing to let God into the mess. And there I stew. Usually without realizing it, I grow more and more resentful toward God for symbolizing all the goodness and perfection that I obviously cannot master. Before long "God" has become an idol, a projection of my own self-condemnation. This idol can have enormous negative power, driving me on to exhausting acts of self-justification, making me brutally impatient with everyone, and separating me by guilt and anger from the mercy of the living God.

Yet in Christ we learn that God is goodness and love itself, and has nothing whatsoever to do with violence, hatred, and anger. You have sinned, but God does not hate you or condemn you; I would even go so far as to say that God does not hate your sinning. God does not need to *hate* sin, for God simply loves it out of its sinfulness and back into real life. But we must also say that whenever we are set *against* Love we are bound to experience Love as working against *us*, even as condemning us. This may be like what many alcoholics feel when they are confronted by family members: they experience the loving concern and action of their family as gross interference, an attack on their freedom and identity. The relentless mercy and love of God, pursuing the fleeing sinner, are liable to seem even more threatening. Having someone love you when you are angry, ashamed, and bitter can be very trying; having infinite Love in your face while you are trying to avoid Love is hell.

All this brings us to our third and last question: What difference does Christ's work make? Salvation means our restoration to the fellowship with God that we were created to enjoy and that alone makes us truly ourselves. That means we have to rule out either of the two extremes in this area. First, salvation is not something that can simply be applied to us externally, like a bandage, because it does its work through our gradually growing to participate more and more fully in God's life. Nor, at the other extreme, is salvation simply an example of how we ought to behave. We cannot "behave" until we are reunited with God, for it is this relationship with God in Christ that *allows* us to act normally, free of fear, anger, pride, and despair. But this renewed relationship is not something we know how—or even want—to rekindle for ourselves.

Archbishop William Temple spoke tellingly of our experience of God's "anger" and the necessity for our participation and transformation through Christ's saving work. Concerning what happens when sin carries us into bitter opposition to God's unwavering love, Temple writes:

> God's Will is set one way and mine is set against it. There is a collision of wills; and God's Will is not passive in that collision. There is an antagonism of God against me—not indeed an ill-will towards me, for what He wills is my good—but most certainly a contrary will actively opposing me. And, therefore, though He longs to forgive, He cannot do so unless either my will is turned from its sinful direction into conformity with His, or else there is at work some power that is capable of effecting that change in me. To forgive is to restore to the old intimacy; there can be no intimacy between God and me in so far as I set my will against His. Moreover, I am only one of His family. He cannot restore me to the freedom of the family if there is ill-will in me against other members of it.[6]

It would be a chilly kind of forgiveness that did nothing to restore "the old intimacy," as Temple puts it. This requires that men and women freely return in love and penitence to full intimacy with God, and this is exactly what we see Christ accomplishing throughout his life. But it also requires that the power and grace of that renewed relationship be poured out in all of us, so that Christ can make his offering of himself to the Father *in us*, drawing us into his restored communion. This is what happens in the sending to us of the Spirit, for the Holy Spirit *is* this infinite intimacy of the Father and the Son, now poured out through Christ into the fellowship of his people.

∼ The Sovereignty of Sacrificial Love

The title for this section is drawn from Archbishop Michael Ramsey's description of the heart of Christianity:

> Jesus gave himself. He would not save himself. He gave himself to share in the deep darkness of a world sinful, estranged. But the apostles of Jesus came to believe that when Jesus died in this manner, giving himself and not saving himself, he was not contradicting the reign of God. Rather was he, the divine Son, showing what the reign of God is like and how the reign of God comes, indeed what God himself is like. In the utter self-giving of Jesus in the desolation of his death there is the divine self-giving love, the very essence of deity.... We believe indeed that God is omnipotent and sovereign. But his is always the sovereignty of self-giving, pain-bearing love. There is no other sovereignty in the universe.[7]

This sovereignty of divine love is what frees us from being subject to any other forces. How? How does Jesus' suffering presence set us free?

Put very simply (and, I fear, in banal terms), the idea is this: Jesus restores our relationship with God. If the fall distorts our desires and turns us into caricatures of what we might be, Jesus forges for us a new way of being human. Through the constant struggle of each temptation overcome, the daily decisions about how best to love, Jesus finds his human fulfillment not in a quest for natural survival but through a continual giving of himself in love to his people and so to God. And this self-giving life is not destroyed in his dying but vindicated in resurrection life. Jesus, we could say, has not just passed through life or suffered death, but has taken them and made of them an offering of himself. He has recreated human personal life by freeing it from the desire to exist on its own terms and restored it from within to its true source: the loving self-sharing that is the pattern of God's own trinitarian life. It is in this sense that we could say Jesus is a sacrifice for sin. He has taken our bitter separation from God into his own life, lived in its midst, loved its victims, and shared its fate. But, in doing so, he has brought all this to the Father; he has made our fearful separation from God into the matter of his prayer, his relationship with God. Nothing, absolutely nothing, not even the worst of human sin or suffering, can be cut off from God any longer.

So salvation is possible not because God has conveyed to the world some useful tips for a more prosperous life, but because in Jesus, God is "risking" being God by being human. We know that it is the joy of God's trinitarian life to be God by being one-with-another, by loving infinitely across "otherness" and difference to enjoy eternal communion. In Christ we see this trinitarian loving able to embrace into its life not only what is "other" to God, our human life, but even what is antagonistic to God, the sin of the world. Because God speaks the divine Word *there*, on the cross, God can be said to overcome all the alienation of the cosmos—entering into the lostness, and from within *transmuting* separation and division into the joyful embrace of fellowship.

In the mission of the Word carried out by Jesus on the cross, God renders violent antagonism into peaceful mutuality. The relationship of Father to Son, that unity we call Holy Spirit, stretches out in aching, suffering love as the Son enters more and more into the condition of our separation from God. At last on the cross, the very being of God's relational life seems stretched to the breaking point: Jesus fully bears in himself the trauma of the world's isolation from God, until finally it seems to him that the Father has forsaken him, that God's love could reach no further into our lostness. The resurrection and outpouring of the Spirit upon us is the overwhelming and life-changing vindication of God's loving, God's trinitarian life, which is able to embrace, take to heart, and forgive the sin of the world.

So far I have been saying three things. First, Jesus' self-giving love forges a new way of being human, a way that allows our personhood to grow into that fullness of life we call communion with God. Second, the events in which this takes place reveal the dark secret of the evil that haunts us like a nightmare, showing it to us, showing even its most sinister ploy—death itself—as overcome and healed in the resurrection of Jesus. As this trusting mind of Christ begins to grow in us, the tyranny of sin and death is destroyed. Sin can no more terrify us into hiding from God. And third, because the act of Jesus' self-sharing love is, as Archbishop Ramsey said, itself the very self-sharing of God, not only our sins but the sins of the whole world become the "matter" for God's self-disclosure. For in Christ, God reveals to us that the love of Father for Son is stronger than death, and capable of stretching over the divisions of the whole creation, embracing all and converting all to fellowship within the uniting power of the Holy Spirit.

So the action of God in Christ for our salvation includes and transforms us all to one degree or another. For the personal pattern of Christ's life is not that of an individual man who happened to be good friends with God. His relationship with the Father, his sonship, is a path of life now open to every human being through baptism into his life. That is what we will explore in the next and final chapter on the mystery of the church and of God's coming kingdom, where the salvation won by Christ overtakes the world and makes a new heaven and a new earth.

Chapter Seven

The Drama of the Cosmos

The Mystery of Communion

> Then I saw a new heaven and a new earth; for
> the first heaven and the first earth had passed
> away, and the sea was no more. And I saw the
> holy city, the new Jerusalem, coming down out
> of heaven from God, prepared as a bride
> adorned for her husband. And I heard a loud
> voice from the throne saying, "See the home of
> God is among mortals. He will dwell with them
> as their God; they will be his peoples, and God
> himself will be with them; he will wipe every
> tear from their eyes."
>
> *Revelation 21:1-4*

Why is God creating you? Why, at this very instant, is God calling into existence the "vast expanse of interstellar space, galaxies, suns, the planets in their courses," as we say in a eucharistic prayer? Scientists now think that beyond our own universe may exist an infinite array of parallel or related universes, a "mulitverse." Why? Why this seemingly infi-

nite fruitfulness, this extravagant unfurling, this
heart-stopping voyage of bare existence onward into
consciousness and love right past all the possible dead
ends and cosmic collapses?

Throughout these chapters our answer has been
that *God creates out of love*. Christians believe that God
continually creates out of love so that all creatures
may share in the divine life, may find home and fullness of life in God's infinite self-sharing. Each creature
that is drawn into God's life becomes a new moment
in the loving of the divine Persons, a gift of God to God
in God. We hear some of this loving conversation of
God's trinitarian life in this passage from John:

> I have made your name known to those whom
> you gave me from the world. They were yours,
> and you gave them to me, and they have kept
> your word. Now they know that everything
> you have given me is from you.... All mine are
> yours, and yours are mine; and I have been glo-
> rified in them.... But now I am coming to you,
> and I speak these things in the world so that
> they may have my joy made complete in them-
> selves. (John 17:6-7, 10, 13)

Here Jesus opens up his life with the Father to his
friends: "I have called you friends, because I have
made known to you everything that I have heard
from my Father" (John 15:15). He lets his disciples in
on the great joy of the divine dialogue. And what they
hear, astonishingly, is something about *themselves*,
namely that they have been made participants, actors,
in the play of eternal giving that is God's life. The disciples hear themselves described as gifts of the loving
Father to the Son, and these living gifts are received by
Jesus—taken into his mission, healed and loved and
broken open, and made to blossom as persons. He sets

us free, he puts our talents to work, he lets us grow into the persons God is inviting us to be. Finally, through his death and resurrection, Jesus gathers his disciples into a community where his mind, his Spirit of relationship with the Father, can be received.

At Pentecost we see this final act of Jesus' ministry. The community he has prepared is now set ablaze by God the Holy Spirit, speaking the Word to the whole world, making the loving offering that is Jesus on behalf of the whole world. In this way, we become the church, Christ's Body, and by the ceaseless renewal of the Spirit's presence we are able to offer "ourselves, our souls and bodies" back to the Father in Christ's own eucharistic self-giving. That is why God has created us, and that is what this chapter is all about: how and why the goal of created life is participation in God's life, a life of eternal, giving love of which the church is the sign in our world.

I believe that Jesus is the beginning of the new creation. Because of who he is, God's eternal Beloved, he is able to fulfill his human existence no longer in the bitter and distorted fashion of this world, but in the manner in which human being was created to exist— in relationship with God. Jesus *is* human existence being drawn into life precisely in that pattern of loving self-sharing which is the relationship of the eternal Son to God the Father. That is *who* Jesus is. And we are called to bring his life into the world's heart, to fill the world with resurrection life. That is what we are as church, the place where the distorted pattern of the world's life is changed into the pattern of Jesus' relationship with the Father.

Suppose as a child you had a knack for music, but for some reason this musical capacity never came alive in you—perhaps your parents could not afford lessons or an instrument, perhaps your friends talked you out of it, or perhaps the slow and agonizing process of becoming a musician, with all its inevitable moments of failure, was just too much for you. And so now, instead of the challenges and delights of belonging to a string quartet and performing music together, you sit alone with a computer synthesizer, piecing together noises into advertising jingles for used car dealerships.

The church is the community where the musician you might have become comes into contact with the mission of Christ, his healing and forgiveness and power to save. The disfigured and stunted pattern of your life, drawn into the trusting pattern of the church's fidelity to Christ, is re-created. It becomes possible for you to repent, to turn away from whatever has kept your talent, your personhood, locked morosely and cautiously away. So you begin to risk playing your cello again and to offer your music to others. More profoundly, through your rediscovered joy you yourself become a gift, an offering, until you finally come to that perfect participation in God's life where you will be God's own music, an offering of joy by God to God in God, an offering of Christ to the Father in their Spirit.

Does this sound hopelessly idealistic? Perhaps. And yet over and over the church has witnessed the liberation of men and women into the freedom of Christ's life, and their gradual blossoming as true persons. On the other hand, wherever participation in the church's life *leaves* individuals in their isolation, their mistrust of themselves and each other, there the church stands condemned as in desperate need of renewal.

I am proposing, then, that in this chapter we think about how we become real, authentic, loving persons and what role the church has in that process. Above all, we will think about the divine joy of communion, whose pattern and rhythm is ultimately nothing less than that eternal event of self-giving love whom we know as God the Blessed Trinity. My hunch is that God's desire to make real persons of us all and God's desire to bring to birth a new creation are the very same desire in God. Who we are becoming and what happens to the world cannot be separated.

∼ Finding Your Role and Purpose in Life

Have you ever tried to write a novel? Really good writers, I am told, so vibrantly invest their characters with life that often the story just seems to "write itself." The plot develops so naturally and spontaneously out of the characteristic habits, interactions, fears, hopes, and loves of the characters that the world of the novel is woven together entirely by the development of its characters.

The livelier and more realistic these characters are, the more the story's world seems to emerge from their own growth and failures, triumphs and reconciliations. So the growth of persons, in this analogy, is crucially significant to the construction and transformation of a whole world of meaning. Why? Because the author's purpose (the story-line) has come to life and is being carried forward by the persons of the story. This story-line is not some unrelated possibility, disconnected from the characters, but the growth and interaction of the characters themselves and the future they bring into being. The end and goal of the story is coming to life in the lives of the characters. In the same way, you are a cherished character in the story God is creating. Your struggles, your loves, your fears, your tears, your laughter, your compassion, your sins—out of these details God is writing the story of the universe.

But now, instead of a novel, what if we were talking about a play, with an author, several actors, and a director?[1] Unlike the characters in a novel (who can at least be "halted" by the author if they start going awry!), the actors in a play are completely involved in the creation of the play and the carrying-out of the playwright's purpose. If they seriously misinterpret their roles, or fail to bring these roles to life, then the play will turn into a grotesque parody of the author's original idea. For the characters in a play, when thoughtfully acted, transform the ideas and words of the author into living meaning. As the actors "become" their roles, they gather up all the possibilities of the story and cause its meaning to grow and change as long as the play goes forward. How they interpret any given moment may transform completely the significance of what happens. And it all depends on how well they become who they are, how well they discover the truth of their character.

This analogy with drama highlights for us the significance of personhood in bringing about meaning. But, even more, it points to how one individual, an actor, can enter with greater and greater perception and clarity into a new role, a new way of being a person. This *persona* of the actor's character in the play can, in a very real sense, bring to light many aspects of the actor's own humanity. Some roles are so remarkably right for some actors that as they live into their parts these actors become more truly themselves. The role galvanizes them by calling forth talents, moods, and insights that have been unused or misused. And in embracing that mission, that character's role, the actor seems more personal, more living, than ever before.

I am sure you know somebody who seems to come to life in certain roles, certain life situations, where you intuitively sense a "rightness" in that person's every word or deed. But how do we discover those "roles" that suit us best, bringing us to life and allowing us to find the truth of ourselves? Perhaps at certain moments in your own life you have felt this possibility more strongly and clearly than at other times—moments when you felt with a deep joy and peacefulness that *this* was what you were made for. But there are also times, lasting for years on end, when we feel we have lost touch with the person we have it in us to become. Usually this happens because our culture or our upbringing has so distorted our sense of ourselves that we no longer can sense the deep longing and desire of God, tugging us toward the truth of ourselves. Then our own fear and hurt condemn us to a lifetime of hesitant and distracted attempts.

It is exactly this pattern of humanity-living-into-personhood that is going on in Jesus' case. His humanity is from its very conception and birth being drawn into that unique personhood through which he will find complete fulfillment as a human being. The more he struggles each day and hour to live out the "role," the identity of God's Beloved, the more he grows into a free and flourishing human being, and the more resoundingly he is the Person of the Word made present in our midst. Think of his hours of prayer, searching out his Father's will, longing with every fibre of his being to be Son to such a Father in every situation the world would throw at him.

Certainly we hear of conflict and agony in Jesus' journey to live out his identity. Our own world bombards us with messages and situations that tug us all, Christ included, away from that relationship with God which is the making of our personhood. We can sense Jesus, like a great actor, struggling to learn how to enact his role, to live into his mission, to speak to others:

> Now my soul is troubled. And what should I say—"Father, save me from this hour"? No, it is for this reason that I have come to this hour. (John 12:27)

"What should I say?" What are the words, the inflection, the movement of my heart that will allow me to *be* who I am most authentically? Over and over, Jesus had to search through each situation, with the guidance and direction of the Holy Spirit leading him into the truth of his identity, showing him how to be the one who comes to do the Father's will on earth as in heaven.

Jesus is not the Person he is by calculating how much love to show—he simply loved and risked being so completely present with and for other persons that his own Personhood was utterly available. Our personhood is not something finished that we harbor within us, but discovered and *lived into* through our relationships—especially those relationships of loving self-giving that seem to call us out of what we *think* of as ourselves into a deeper and bolder identity. In the same way Jesus' Personhood, while always alive in him, was not his private possession but the ongoing gift to him of the Father's love. In our world, this gift of the Father takes the form of the giving of the disciples to Jesus—his Personhood is always, so to speak, "out there"; it is discovered and enacted in the details of his encounters with those whom the Father has given him. It is in loving his people to the end that Jesus fulfills his personal identity and knows himself as God's Beloved. And our personhood is created through, and in, and for this same relationship.

~ **Losing Touch with our Roles**

Because of the danger and fearfulness that inhibit our journey toward personhood, we suffer from a grievous loneliness. It is hard to risk those authentic relationships with others in which the words God gives us could find their deepest meaning. Insofar as we draw back from real relationships with each other, we fade away as persons. We are afraid to risk true presence to each other, and so our speaking and acting no longer link us with each other as deeply as we yearn for. Our words and acts themselves become artificial, vacant, mere gestures without meaning. Think of how painful it is when you have been hurt by someone but have to go to a meeting with him or her; you smile outwardly and protect yourself inwardly, gradually sealing yourself off from the one who hurt you until all that is left is for you to endure the same physical space together. Moreover, the same sin that eats away at our relationships also infects the structures of the world around us, negating our words and embraces, our very means for communion, or else turning them into weapons. When we hide from each other, then the world we inhabit is no longer filled with the meaning-making task of trying to live and communicate with each other.

To return to the analogy of drama for a moment, I once had a part in an eighth-grade musical. All of us had to speak lines whose range of meaning and emotion was far beyond our comprehension, and for that very reason we descended into adolescent farce. Speaking for myself, there was no way I could have lent my own experiences (how I wished I had had some!) of being a debonair lover to my part, and I was *far* too frightened to risk exposing my true inexperience. None of us knew how to risk the kind of relationships our roles called for, so we just acted, we pretended, and none of us were able to help the other to grow into the reality of our roles. We merely mouthed the words back and forth, making noises whose potential significance we could not have even guessed.

It strikes me how similar our situation is to that eighth-grade musical: the language, the props, the relationships, the encounters, the very stage itself of God's drama. Through sin the drama has become clumsy and forced, its meaning emptied out and long forgotten, its potential unrealized, its hopes trivialized. How little we know what the world is *for*. Most of us engage in benign or humdrum exploitation of the world around us. But if we grow up in poverty or a war zone, or have our house daubed with swastikas or our church burned down or our children terrorized in school, we have little illusion about the world's lethal misdirection of purpose.

Besides these individual and social dimensions, there is also the more cosmic level. For if our common life is no longer able to draw us out into personhood, at the same time we are increasingly unable to give the world its true meaning because sin has warped and enfeebled our performance. We do not have the freedom and loving authenticity to act out that divine drama in which the world's true meaning and purpose would come to light. In the repetitive and increasingly violent routines we have been reduced to, God's beautiful creation becomes either a rag bag of objects for our own exploitation or a collection of idols before which we prostrate ourselves, which comes to the same thing. We are not like actors who understand their roles and the transcendent purpose of the play. An actor who is really living the part is able to turn what was a mere stage prop into something significant and meaningful: a wet, bedraggled bit of felt becomes a hat; the hat, worn with a certain *élan*, becomes the image of someone's courage or hope. A good actor can invest a mere item with the life that comes from playing its own particular role in the play's unfolding.

Think of those little bits and pieces of creation that have found their way into your life. To someone else they appear ordinary, devoid of any deep significance, but because they have been taken up into your story they are priceless, heartbreaking: a shell you found and brought home from your first trip to the beach, the glasses your father wore the year he died, the scent of wind and rain the night you first kissed. Or simple bread and wine taken up into a meal, and that meal itself taken up in Christ's hands, blessed and broken, given back to us with a meaning that would re-create this world into a new one, a new relationship, a new covenant.

To bear the creation up into the crucible of God's plan, where its meaning and significance can become radiant and transforming, requires the authority of one who knows what the play is all about. If we do not know how to grow into true persons, how can we turn matter into meaning and let it shine, illumined by the divine purposes into which we might have brought it? No wonder the whole "creation waits with eager longing for the revealing of the children of God . . . , in hope that the creation itself will be set free from its bondage to decay and will obtain the freedom of the glory of the children of God" (Romans 8:19-21). Because we no longer know how to be persons, how to live as the children of God by offering ourselves, each other, and our world into the divine life of eternal giving and receiving love, the world around us is no longer free to grow into all that it could be. Subject to deterioration and misuse, it is no longer sacramental, transparent to God, or capable of being alive as an element in the divine glory.

But the drama of God's cosmos will not be dissolved into meaningless squeaks in a darkened, emptied theater. No, the whole creation, the whole drama must be made new—not by simply obliterating the old, but by drawing it into the new. And so the central meaning of the drama, the Word whose relationship with the Father undergirds the very existence of every creature, is reenacted in the midst of the chaos we have made. Jesus enacts for us the relationship with God by which we are all drawn into true personhood. It is in finding our particular, unique share in his role, in living into his mission, that we begin to unfold and blossom as persons once more ourselves—no longer self-conscious or embarrassed, but free and clear and alive with God's calling to us. John's gospel says, "To all who received him, who believed in his name, he gave the power to become children of God, who were born, not of blood or of the will of the flesh or of the will of man, but of God" (John 1:12-13). We are to be reborn and completed as human beings not in terms of biological necessity or the willful distortions of sinful human society ("not of blood or of the will of the flesh"), but as true *persons.*

ᨆ Becoming New Persons in the Church

So far we have been thinking about the relationship between our growth as true persons and the journey of the whole creation toward its God-given end. We have considered our grace-given potential to draw each other into the fullness of reality, the meaning of God's story, but we have also seen how our hurt and broken world makes it increasingly difficult for us to discover our true roles, to embrace them with the freedom, trust, and joy that could really bring them to life. You might imagine the human race as a broken-down band of third-rate actors, rehearsing over and over again fragments of unrelated plays, each acting out his or her own little drama but never connecting. At times we are hopeful when we seem for a moment actually to be speaking with one another, moving into conversation, making meaning, only to lapse back into our separate routines.

Now, what if someone came among us with such a passion for his role that he truly lived it out? What if we saw someone who did not just "act out" sadness or compassion or joy, but who actually lived as though he stood for something, as though he was connected to something larger than himself? We might fall in with this itinerant player. If we did, the momentum and exuberance of his story would begin to sweep all our fragmented and lonely acts into a great drama, and in his drama our stories would find at last their meaning and coherence ("Ah, *that's* what I've always wanted to do!"). Before we know it, our individual routines turn out to have a significant effect on others because someone is weaving us into a drama with a real meaning, a goal, a hope, a consummation. Think of the apostle Peter, who kept trying to go fishing with a ludicrous lack of success but then discovered the real point of his impulse to go fishing:

> As Jesus passed along the Sea of Galilee, he saw Simon and his brother Andrew casting a net into the sea—for they were fishermen. And Jesus said to them, "Follow me and I will make you fish for people." (Mark 1:16-17)

In his earthly ministry Jesus seems to have done this over and over again, so that men and women, in companionship with him, could begin at last to glimpse the true meaning and purpose of their lives.

He gave them a sense of who they had it in them to become, and where their destinies would take them. This was far from haphazard: Jesus carefully unfolds his mission and identity in the lives of the people he gathers around him. Their growth as a new people is, in a crucial sense, the very center of his mission. He takes some of them with him when he visits the sick; he explains parables to them; he asks them about their own understanding of his work; he implores them to pray, to have faith, to keep watch with him. In short, he works to refashion their identity. It is as though he is drawing them into a way of being human that is larger than all of them together, a corporate personhood, a communal Life.

So Jesus seems to have been intentionally forming a community. By structuring his community around "the twelve," Jesus was signalling that their own identity as *God's people*, as the twelve tribes of Israel whom God called into covenant, was about to be renewed. Jesus expected that his mission and destiny would call the twelve together in a new and powerful way, as witnesses to the new work God is bringing to pass. For this reason he deliberately sent out a representative group of twelve apostles ("apostle" is from the Greek verb *apostello*, to send) as witnesses to God's new work. Think, for example, of how these twelve become Christ's agents in feeding the new pilgrim people of God in stories of loaves and fishes, bearing Jesus' own personal pattern of life into the community's life.

Why does Jesus carry out his mission by forming a community? Why could he not simply minister to separate individuals, imparting wisdom to each as they needed it? Because what Jesus embodies in our midst is God's Word, God's self-expression. God is no super-individual, but the communion of the Blessed

Trinity. So for Jesus to embody *God's* life in the midst of *our* life means breaking down our violent and fearful ways of being together and replacing them with the peaceful self-giving of God's way of being "together."

Sometimes when my two children are squabbling I get so frustrated and embroiled that I end up acting just as badly as they do by shouting, arguing, trying to assert my judgment over theirs. And that is what our world does: it sucks us into its conflicts with a kind of hypnotic power, mesmerizing us into acting a certain way, into becoming a certain kind of person with this kind of job and that kind of life. Sometimes the suggestions are alluring and beautiful—a glossy magazine or an enthralling movie; sometimes they take a more brutal and shocking form, arousing in us a primitive desire for more and more violence, calling into being a self who lives to compete, to win, to fight, to annihilate. Played any video games lately? Or how about the stock market?

Remember how often in the gospels various people try to draw Jesus into their arguments, their conflicts and ways of seeing things:

> Somone in the crowd said to him, "Teacher, tell my brother to divide the family inheritance with me." But he said to him, "Friend, who set me to be a judge or arbitrator over you?" (Luke 12:13-14)

The prince of this world would like very much to draw Jesus into the whole cycle of rivalry, fear, and antagonism. But Jesus, as we see, has a different response. Just so, in my saner moments, instead of getting trapped in my children's fighting, I remember to say, "Who wants to go to the library?" or (if I am desperate) "Who wants to go out for ice cream?" While it may seem I am distracting my children, in fact I am trying, however feebly, to redirect their desire. This is not so far from what Jesus does. He creates an environment, a community, in which people's desires can be redirected toward the only real satisfaction of that desire, God.[2]

How does he do this? Not merely by *preaching* about the kingdom and the Father, although that is crucial, but above all by letting his friends *in* on his own desire, his relationship with the Father. He tells them things and takes them out to pray and shows them the beauty of God's creative hand, "so that my joy may be in you, and that your joy may be complete" (John 15:11). Because Jesus' own identity is ceaselessly loved into being by the Father, he can rescue us from the world. He puts his hands on our heads and directs our gaze right through the world's antic posing to the One who loves him, and thus he suggests to each of us a new identity, one that is able to share with him in the endless blessedness of being God's beloved.

This process by which Jesus calls new personhood into being takes place throughout his ministry, but especially by his forgiving presence as victim—crucified and yet more alive than ever with God's love for us. My own experience is that it is in those moments when, perhaps painfully, we allow Christ to show us how entirely he forgives us, how utterly we are loved, that we begin to sense a new and cherished identity coming to birth in us. Think of the many different ways in which he speaks to us of the Father, imbuing us with his own trust and confidence in the Father and creating in us the love that casts out all fear:

> Consider the ravens: they neither sow nor reap,
> they have neither storehouse nor barn, and yet
> God feeds them. Of how much more value are

you than the birds!...And do not keep striving for what you are to eat and what you are to drink, and do not keep worrying. For it is the nations of the world that strive after all these things, and your Father knows that you need them. Instead, strive for his kingdom, and these things will be given to you as well. Do not be afraid, little flock, for it is your Father's good pleasure to give you the kingdom. (Luke 12:24, 29-32)

Throughout Christianity's history there has been a tendency to understand following Christ as the extinction or suppression of our desire. But Jesus seems to have been more interested in *unlocking* our desire, breaking it loose from the anxious, fearful, obsessive desire we see in the world around us, and setting it ablaze with God's own desire. A particularly famous and beautiful example of this inflaming of our desire as the re-creation of our personhood comes from a passage in Augustine's *Confessions*. Augustine is lamenting how easily he was hoodwinked into trying to satisfy his desire with the things of this world. But then he praises God for arousing him to an even greater desire:

You have called to me, and have cried out, and have shattered my deafness. You have blazed forth with light, and have shone upon me, and you have put my blindness to flight! You have sent forth your fragrance, and I have drawn in my breath, and I pant after you. I have tasted you, and I hunger and thirst after you. You have touched me, and I have burned for your peace.[3]

God's outpouring of the divine life initiates a recipro-
cal yearning in Augustine. But notice how God does
this—not by simply giving Augustine a gift to possess,
albeit a divine gift, but rather by awakening all his
senses, all the structures of Augustine's self. God, we
could say, re-creates Augustine by awakening an "I"
who lives by the desire for God. Augustine describes
himself as one whose senses have been restored to
their true functions; he is more alive than ever as a
person *because* he is alive in response to and in relationship with God.

As I have suggested before, this desire that the
Father pours out and the Son opens our hearts to
receive is none other than God the Holy Spirit, becoming the soul of our soul, the spirit of our spirit. But
this does not happen to us *privately*; it takes place in
and through the communion of new relationships we
call the church. Why? Because God's life is a *communal* event of loving, the Trinity, and therefore it cannot
come among us without taking a communal form.
Indeed, the Father loves Jesus into being by giving him
others to love in turn—disciples to teach, the broken-
hearted to comfort, and the world to save. It is precisely by going out of himself in love toward all these
others that Jesus is most himself, the Beloved of God.
In the same way we become most ourselves through
participation in Jesus' relationship with the Father,
and that relationship takes the form of a glorious,
struggling, comically (and sometimes tragically) inept
community of disciples.

At Pentecost the Holy Spirit descends upon this collection of individuals and, like a good theater director,
draws each of us into his or her particular role in
Jesus' mission. Just as Jesus is the person he is by
means of his self-giving for others, so we are brought
to a new identity through the new patterns of self-

giving that become available to us in the church. As the Spirit overshadows us and re-members us into Christ's Body, we are called into personhood through our fellowship with each other. Every adult forum, Christmas bazaar, youth group retreat, vestry meeting, soup kitchen clean-up, hospital visit, door-to-door calling, every-member canvass, abandoned building reclamation, Bible study, home church meeting—all have been "sealed by the Holy Spirit in baptism and marked as Christ's own forever." Every detail of our common life has the potential to knit us together into the new creation.

For that to be possible the church needs to nourish us in repentance, turning us toward our authentic vocation. The particular *you* that God is bringing to life is not someone whose past is lost or meaningless, but one whose whole life is now free and available for others. I think how often I have come to church with my heart still wounded and trapped in some quandary; I am there but I am not there. By grim determination I may be able to blot out what has happened, but then I come to church as a ghost, a pale phantom who is only pretending to be a person. In repentance we turn away from this half-life toward the one who calls us out of our tombs. In repentance we begin to sense how our lives, with all their sins and hurts and ugly places, are embraced by God and, in time, woven uniquely into the divine design.

Rowan Williams comments on how these converted selves, our persons-in-the-making, are called into life by sharing in the church's giving life:

> My charism, the gift given me to give to the community, is my *self*, ultimately; my story given back, to give me a place in the net of exchange, the web of gifts, which is Christ's

Church. My self is to be given away in love, not
because it is worthless, but because it is
supremely precious, given to me by the hand of
God as he returns my memory. Out of my
story, the Spirit of the risen Jesus constitutes
my present possibilities of understanding, compassion, and self-sharing. . . . [Earlier] we considered the state of "fallen" humanity in terms
of a chain of mutual deprivation, robbery with
violence: here we see how "redeemed" humanity inverts this system into a chain of mutual
gift, exchange of life. And the pivot is the learning of one's own self as gift, allowing it to be
returned—whatever the initial pain or shame—
by the risen Christ, hearing one's true name
from his lips.[4]

This receiving of myself as a gift to be given is not, I
find, something that one gets the hang of all at once.
The "me" that the world has called into being struggles for indulgence and against real growth in self-
giving—murmuring to keep myself safe, not to risk
loving where I might get hurt, not to put myself out,
not to forgive. But the church is exactly the place
where we can all practice this giving life together,
where we can look at each other—brothers and sisters
for whom Christ died—and hope to find at last someone willing to receive patiently, forgivingly, but hon-
estly the gift of ourselves.

～ Making Eucharist of the World
Now it is time, at last, to see how all this might help
us to think about the final sovereignty of God and the
creation of a new world. Throughout the chapter I
have been trying to connect a few points, stars in a
night sky, to see what kind of picture they might

make. We have seen that Jesus' Personhood is the expression of his relationship with the Father and he has called us to share in that relationship. We become authentic persons ourselves as we enter into that trinitarian life of giving love, and Jesus' forming of us into a community is essential to his mission. Only a community can embody on earth something of that eternal communion which is the life of heaven.

Our dramatic analogy has helped us to imagine how it is that we are drawn into ever more vibrant personhood as we live into God's calling, God's unique "role" for each of us. Furthermore, we have seen how our mutual journey toward the truth of our identities in Christ is inextricably bound up with the destiny of the creation itself. For it is our task, as creatures made in the image of God, to bring the rest of creation into its own meaning and final consummation, to render creation transparent to God, ablaze with God's glory. We are the particular creatures in which the whole creation can consciously, intentionally, and freely offer itself once more to God. In us the bare matter of the universe has grown into mindful, compassionate personhood, capable of giving self away in love and freedom to another. In Christ, God initiated this self-giving of the creation by restoring to humanity our intimacy with God and the confidence to commend ourselves once more entirely into the hands of our Father, without shame or fear: "Father, into your hands I commend my spirit" (Luke 23:46). And so, in Jesus the self-giving return of the whole creation to God has definitively begun, and now, by the power of the Spirit, Christ offers more and more of the world to the Father through his Body the church.

The broken world we live in is characterized by deprivation, fear, and the violent urge to seize existence for ourselves; the new creation flows directly from the one "who, though he was in the form of God, did not regard equality with God as something to be exploited, but emptied himself" (Philippians 2:6–7). Jesus is able to live our humanity into fruition because he knows that there is not a finite amount of love to be possessed, but always more and more of it to share. Most important of all, Jesus breathes into his community the knowledge that the eternal self-giving of love is set loose in our world by the one act our world fears the most: giving ourselves away freely in loving trust to another.

The fixed economy of death in which we live is not the result of a *shortage* of life and love, so that the only hope is to grab life away from someone else. No, our fearful world is the result of an unwillingness to let love *flow*. It is the result of a frantic effort to sustain ourselves *by* ourselves and on our own, apart from communion with God. This communion always seems risky and frightening because the divine life is like a vast abyss of self-giving; to enter that abyss, we fear, would be the end of us. And indeed it would be— the end of the frightened and exhausted "I" who has been called into being by this world, but the beginning of a new "I," a new self.

Simone Weil wrote movingly of this secret of existence where "to be" most fully is to "be *for another.*" To be oneself at last is to be given into the embrace of another, to be free for the loving of God:

> Our existence is made up only of [God's] waiting for our acceptance not to exist. He is perpetually begging from us that existence which he gives. He gives it only to beg it from us.[5]

Weil, in arrestingly dramatic language, is saying that behind and beneath the false "I" that the world has concocted there exists a truer and more wonderful person who is ceaselessly being called into life by the self-giving love of God.

But this true person exists only in the image of the divine existence, and *that* existence, as we know from the mystery of the Holy Trinity, is constituted by the eternal giving away of life One to Another. "We have to die," says Simone Weil, "in order to liberate a *tied up* energy, in order to possess an energy which is free and capable of understanding the true relationship of things."[6] She speaks of the *freeing up* of a life that has been constrained, wasted, exhausted in self-preservation. Or, in more familiar words, "Those who want to save their life will lose it, and those who lose their life for my sake, and for the sake of the gospel, will save it" (Mark 8:35).

In Christ's self-offering, I would suggest, God draws the whole creation more and more into correspondence with the trinitarian offering of God's own life. The self-offering of all creatures to one another and to God becomes transparent to the self-offering of the three divine Persons. We see a hint of this coming transfiguration in St. Paul's conviction that "all of us, with unveiled faces, seeing the glory of the Lord as though reflected in a mirror, are being transformed into the same image from one degree of glory to another" (2 Corinthians 3:18). What we are trying to imagine is a pattern of life in which the whole creation offers itself to God through the free and loving offering of the human community of persons—a self-giving community that the church both represents and draws the world into, so that it becomes attuned to the trinitarian self-giving of God. As that harmonization takes place, the divine glory is seen in the transfiguration of creation, in its perfect self-surrender to God.

This transfiguration is hard to imagine, but surely we see it happening in parable even now. A pile of sand is taken up into the imagination of a child, the grains are set in motion and transformed into a castle. The painful disjointed pieces of a novelist's own life are offered, like wood to a fire, to the artistry of the novel, and out of her own suffering she brings forth a story that speaks life-giving truth. Jesus invites us into his own heart, into the passion of divinely giving love, and transfigures us into a sign of his resurrection.

And that is only the beginning. In his death and resurrection Jesus confronts the disciples with the Father's love, and in forgiving them he imbues them with a new life no longer fettered by the fear of death. In the sending of the Holy Spirit, God forms this apostolic group into a community that can express not merely Jesus' teachings but his relationship with the Father. Just as Jesus takes up the bread and wine of the community's meal to become his own self-communication ("This is my body, which is given for you"), so too Jesus takes up the disciples—giving them this new eucharistic heart—as the bodily expression of his life with the Father.

The church is called into being as the embodiment of these two fundamental elements in the pattern of Christ's life: Jesus' receiving of his *Personhood*, his identity, from the Father, and Jesus' *offering* of himself to the Father. In this process, the coming of the Holy Spirit is not a kind of consolation prize for the church, but the actual power of that loving communion between the Father and Christ now poured out upon us: the power to make us *persons* of communion and to *offer* the creation back to the Father in trust and joy.

Notice this two-beat pulse of the church's sacramental heart. There is the *baptismal moment* in which the creation is called, through participation in the dying and rising of Christ, into the freedom of new personhood. And there is the *eucharistic moment* when the church, now acting as the "personalized" face of creation, bears creation itself up into the self-offering of Christ, restoring the whole cosmos to a state of communion with God. So in our churchly pilgrimage from baptism to eucharist, we are constantly allowing the Spirit to transform our lives and our world from *possession* to *gift*, from something controlled and hoarded into something free and flowing.

If you have ever been to a child's birthday party, you will know exactly what I am talking about. In one of the classic devices used by party "experts" to torment parents, each child is given a puzzle piece upon arrival at the party. In the ensuing happy play, the party experts announce, the children will discover to their delight that they are holding pieces to a common puzzle and will sit down together in a charmingly cooperative spirit to put the puzzle picture together. You can imagine what *really* happens: it soon becomes apparent to all the children that everyone else has a different, and obviously much better, puzzle piece. Soon they are all stampeding with anxiety-driven belligerence toward chaotic frenzy, attempting to get all the other pieces for themselves or at least to make sure no one else does, while parents are left with the daunting task of soothing the confusion. Usually this can be done by distracting the frenzy toward the promise of birthday cake; in effect, they call the fearful, squabbling chaos back into something vaguely resembling human persons. And by calling these children to their new identity as cheerful birthday cake recipients, the parents make it possible for the children to release their vicious little grips on the puzzle pieces. They offer them up and, *voilà*, the pieces can at last be put together on the very table at which all the formerly violent puzzle-makers are now feasting happily on cake.

Our world, which God has destined for participation in communion, turned its glories into broken, hoarded fragments—puzzle pieces whose meaning could never be revealed so long as each was grasped in fearful isolation. Jesus enters this confusion and begins to call it back into personal life, one inspired not by birthday cake but by an infinitely higher kind of celebration: the eternal feast of divine communion. As Christ calls us out of our chaos and into personal relationship we are able at last to set creation free, to offer it back to be the very picture, the icon, of God's own abundant life.

Anglican priest and physicist John Polkinghorne suggests that such a cosmic vision is not as fanciful as it might seem. It is true that the matter of this world is characterized by evolutionary struggle, by the painful, costly isolation of self-making, as each species battles for survival. But what if God were to bring about a new pattern of interaction between the universe and God?

> The new creation represents the transformation of that universe when it enters freely into a new and closer relationship with its Creator, so that it becomes a totally sacramental world, suffused with the divine presence. Its process can be free from suffering, for it is conceivable that the divinely ordained laws of nature appropriate to a world making itself through its own evolving history should give way to a differently constituted form of "matter," appropriate to a universe "freely returned" from independence to an existence of integration with its Creator.[7]

Or we could say that the universe is being drawn into a life patterned after Christ's communion with the Father, relationships of trusting self-giving and love rather than grasping, violence, and isolation. Polkinghorne speculates that such a transformation would be felt not only at the personal and social levels—where I believe it is already beginning in the church—but at the level of matter itself. In other words, the church is led by the Spirit to draw the whole world into the transforming power of Christ's relationship with the Father. It is this trinitarian pattern of life that begins to shine and radiate through the renewed pattern of the world's life. One powerful example of this illumination of our world by the world to come is Jesus' transfiguration, where his followers witness the power they will meet in full force at the resurrection. In Jesus' transfiguration the infinite sharing in God's giving life is a form of radiance that illuminates our world, sets it ablaze, makes it translucent and open to the light of God's life.

Two features of the transfiguration stories in the gospels are especially intriguing. First, they set the transfiguration in the context of Jesus' mission: his journey to Jerusalem and his self-offering there. Second, the transfiguration suggests that far from evaporating, his physical presence can itself *become* the shining form of God's life in this world. The first feature (personal mission and commitment) reminds us that this process of transfiguration takes place in and through our renewal as persons—persons who freely give ourselves to our mission in Christ. The second feature (the radiant physical presence of Jesus) highlights the fact that the matter and stuff of our world is not in itself intractable. In Jesus' case it is taken up into the personal act of self-giving, and in that way its very meaning as material stuff of this world is changed, opened up to the indwelling of God's glory.

Thus in Jesus human existence is no longer subordinated to the paralyzing necessity of self-preservation. Rather, Jesus lives his humanity into full personhood and relationship with God, so his humanity itself becomes a radiant sacrament of that self-giving divine life. His human existence is no longer frozen into a mere *thing*, and so its expressive potential is no longer short-circuited by fear. Why? Because in Jesus human existence is "personalized," gathered up into meaning, by being given away in love and freedom. Have you ever seen a maple tree on a dark gray October day? It has a dull and opaque beauty. But if suddenly the sun breaks through the clouds and irradiates all the colors of the leaves with light, then they burst into life, ablaze with an unbelievable power. I think that is what it must have been like to know Jesus in his earthly life. His humanity was not shut down or silenced as ours is, but held up and offered into the radiant light of God's eternal self-giving, rendered glorious and living.

What we see happening dramatically in Jesus' life we can also begin to see in our own. Think of how someone's individual gifts are sometimes set free through the call of Christ. Perhaps a man takes the risk of making himself more and more available to God. As he moves to a new sense of clarity about his mission, his gifts are plunged into the dying and rising of Christ; his provisional selfhood is set free from years of half-use or misuse, and he starts to become the person God had called him to be. Not only does he grow as a person through the call of his baptism, but his renewed identity, with all its gifts, is enlarged and magnified in company with other Christians. Together with them he enters into the eucharist that Christ makes of our world, bringing the world into the self-offering of God, transforming matter into new meaning. This is how the world, as "personified," becomes communion. The eucharist is not merely a symbolic enactment but *is* this event at its consummate moment. The eucharist is the moment in which the world, by the power of the Spirit, becomes *communion*.

Dominican theologian Herbert McCabe has thought this matter through with great clarity, so let me paraphrase his reading of all this.[8] God created the universe to share in the divine communion. But God's call to communion, as we have seen, does not hover securely outside our world or our lives. God offers this communion with us here and now: Jesus *is* this offer of communion, he is the Father's self-bestowing in our midst. In the broken and violent structures of our world, Jesus offered himself as a new means of communication between humans. His life of communion with the Father, the life that we call the Holy Spirit, Jesus put into our hands. He invites us to share in it, to be liberated from sin, death, fear, violence, oppression, and degradation and to be transformed through his life of peaceful communion and trust. As we know, the world tried to get rid of Jesus' kind of friendship, to put it to death and condemn it as a form of wicked blasphemy against God. But the resurrection revealed that the kind of life that Jesus offered, far from blasphemous, is the Father's own self-giving life *expressed* in human terms—a life which, by the Father's own design, simply *embraces* death and goes on living ever more fully and vibrantly.

The resurrection and the forming of the church by the Spirit's advent also makes it possible for us to see what Jesus' life of communion looked like as it became the surrounding matrix for more and more of the world. The forming of the Christian community into Jesus' Body and the extension of his way of life beyond all boundaries of race and nation, provide a hint of how the structures of this world's life might be taken up and transformed into the pattern of God's life. The habits of the world are embraced within Christian love; the world's structures of fear and domination are turned into patterns of solidarity and mutual support. The world does not become less real, it becomes more "worldly" than ever—more itself, more the sacrament of divine communion it was created to be.

This is an extension of what we see happening in the eucharist. Just begin with the physical: here are two batches of chemicals, bread and wine. But these particular molecules are taken up by humans as a means of sharing in life together; not "just" chemicals, but food, and when they are taken up into a meal shared with friends they play the role of communication among human beings. So when Jesus offers himself as a new and radical form of communication among us he is more perfectly "food and drink," more perfectly a means of sharing life together, than even bread and wine. That is why Jesus says in John's gospel that he is the true bread that comes down from heaven: "Since he is the true medium in which we finally meet each other, in which we are finally able to communicate ourselves to each other, he is more intensely food than meat and drink can be."[9] He has taken the things of our world and drawn them into his life, making them a medium of his life. Just so in a more social sense he takes the "elements" of our cultures and societies up into his life as the church, and pours out a new and unfathomably greater kind of culture, a society of trinitarian life.

But just as the eucharist looks very much like ordinary bread and wine even though it is the medium of

Jesus' own self-communication, so too the church can look very much like the ordinary world (sometimes disappointingly so). The eucharist is only a sacrament of Christ's self-giving presence, and the church itself is only a sacrament of the Trinity's self-sharing community. Sacraments are poignant reminders of our separation from God, for they are only the words and the stuff of our world that God uses to speak to us of the world to come.

As such we are in grave danger of idolatry if we try to pretend that our sacramental life is the reality. Throughout history, the church has managed to do some mortally foolish things by forgetting that it is only the sign of God's coming kingdom and not the kingdom itself.

> Christ is, indeed, to be found in the present but precisely as what is rejected by the present world, in the poor and despised and oppressed, he is to be found in those who _unmask_ the present world, those in whom the meaninglessness and inhumanity and contradictions of our society are exposed. Christ will only be, so to say, at home in the world, in the kingdom of the future: it will then be possible to express the exchange of love which is God directly in our bodily lives, simply as our human existence, in the language of what will then be the present.[10]

Perhaps this is close to the meaning of those mysterious and astonishing words in the first letter of John: "Beloved, we are God's children now; what we will be has not yet been revealed. What we do know is this: when he is revealed, we will be like him, for we will see him as he is" (1 John 3:2). At the coming of the kingdom we will be like God; then at last God's life will be the life we lead. Then the exchange of love between all creatures will participate completely in God's exchange of love, the Holy Spirit. Sacraments shall cease, for God's communion will be accomplished ceaselessly and perfectly in the life of every creature. The whole cosmos will be the gift given by the Father to the Son, and offered lovingly by the Son in the eternal jubilation who is the Holy Spirit.

Endnotes

∼ **Chapter 1: Mysteries of Faith**

1. C. S. Lewis, "The Weight of Glory," in *The Weight of Glory and Other Addresses*, (1949; rev. paperback ed., New York: Macmillan, 1980), 18-19.

2. Evagrius of Pontus, *Treatise on Prayer*, 61, quoted in Andrew Louth, *The Origins of the Christian Mystical Tradition: From Plato to Denys* (Oxford: Oxford University Press, 1981), 111. Louth's entire discussion of the interweaving of theology and contemplation in Christianity's formative period is highly informative.

3. Rowan Williams, *The Wound of Knowledge: Christian Spirituality from the New Testament to St. John of the Cross*, 2nd ed. (Cambridge, Mass.: Cowley Publications, 1991), 14.

∼ **Chapter 2: The New Encounter with God**

1. Lewis, "The Weight of Glory," in *The Weight of Glory*, 17.

2. Herbert McCabe, *God Matters* (London: Geoffrey Chapman, 1987), 220.

3. Simone Weil, *Waiting for God*, trans. Emma Craufurd (New York: Harper & Row, 1973), 123-124.

4. Elizabeth Johnson, *She Who Is: The Mystery of God in Feminist Theological Discourse* (New York: Crossroad, 1993), 265.
5. Leonard Hodgson, *Christian Faith and Practice* (Grand Rapids: Eerdmans, 1965), 75.
6. *Ibid.*, 76–77.
7. McCabe, *God Matters*, 224.

～ **Chapter 3: The Splendor of God**
1. Hadewijch, Letter 22, in *The Complete Works*, trans. Columba Hart, OSB, The Classics of Western Spirituality (New York: Paulist Press, 1980), 98.
2. Dorothy L. Sayers, *The Mind of the Maker* (New York: Harper & Row, 1979).

～ **Chapter 4: The Voice of God**
1. Thomas Traherne, *Centuries* (Oxford: The Clarendon Press, 1960; reprint ed., A. R. Mowbray, 1985), 13–14.
2. William Temple, *Nature, Man and God* (1934; London: Macmillan, 1956), 305–306.
3. Konrad Celtis, speaking in his inaugural lecture as a professor at the University of Ingolstadt, quoted in Louis Dupré, *Passage to Modernity: An Essay in the Hermeneutics of Nature and Culture* (New Haven and London: Yale University Press, 1993), 262, note 11.
4. Hymn 661 in *The Hymnal 1982* (New York: Church Hymnal Corporation, 1985). Words by William Alexander Percy.
5. Austin Farrer, sermon entitled "A Share in the Family," in *A Celebration of Faith* (London: Hodder and Stoughton, 1970), 104–105.
6. McCabe, *God Matters*, 20.
7. Hans W. Frei, "Of the Resurrection of Christ," essay in *Theology and Narrative: Selected Essays*, ed. George Hunsinger and William C. Placher (New York: Oxford

University Press, 1993), 203. For Frei's historical and theological accounts of this approach see his works *The Eclipse of the Biblical Narrative* (New Haven: Yale University Press, 1974) and *The Identity of Jesus Christ* (Philadelphia: Fortress, 1975).

~ **Chapter 5: The Humanity of God**

1. John Neville Figgis, *Antichrist and Other Sermons* (London: Longmans, Green and Co., 1913), 77–78.
2. See the useful summaries of these kind of objections in Richard Sturch, *The Word and the Christ: An Essay in Analytic Christology* (Oxford: Oxford University Press, 1991), 17–25.
3. John Hick, *The Myth of God Incarnate* (London: SCM Press, 1977), 178.
4. John Henry Newman, "The Humiliation of the Eternal Son" in *Parochial and Plain Sermons*, vol. 3 (1836; San Francisco: Ignatius Press, 1987), 586–587.
5. Austin Farrer, "Incarnation" in *The Brink of Mystery*, ed. Charles C. Conti (London: SPCK, 1976), 20.

~ **Chapter 6: The Glory of Humanity**

1. Cormac McCarthy, *All the Pretty Horses* (New York: Vintage Books, 1993), 282.
2. James Alison, *Raising Abel: The Recovery of the Eschatological Imagination* (New York: Crossroad, 1996), 26–27.
3. *Ibid.*, 27.
4. Christos Yannaras, *Elements of Faith: An Introduction to Orthodox Theology*, trans. Keith Schram (Edinburgh: T & T Clark, 1991), 112–113.
5. Johnson, *She Who Is*, 158–159.
6. William Temple, *Christus Veritas: An Essay* (London: Macmillan, 1954), 258–259. In this wonderful, if sometimes elusive, book Temple does in fact speak about God's hatred, wrath, and anger at sin, though I

would maintain that the resurrection vindicates God as being utterly unconnected to such states of will. Temple does have this to say about the idea of God's anger at sin: "It is not anger, if by anger we mean the emotional reaction of an offended self-concern; it is anger, if by anger we mean the resolute and relentless opposition of a will set on righteousness against a will directed elsewhere. God must abolish all sinners; but He seeks to abolish sinners by winning them out of their sin into the loyalty and love of children in their Father's home" (*Ibid.*, 259).

7. Michael Ramsey, *To Believe is to Pray: Readings from Michael Ramsey*, ed. James E. Griffiss (Cambridge, Mass.: Cowley Publications, 1996), 137-138.

~ Chapter 7: The Drama of the Cosmos

1. Throughout this chapter I have been greatly helped by the creative use of drama as a metaphor for thinking about theology. This approach has been adopted most profoundly by the Swiss Catholic writer Hans Urs von Balthasar. See his fascinating if challenging five-volume work, *Theo-Drama* (San Francisco: Ignatius Press, 1988–1998). For an introduction to his thought, see my book, *Christology from Within: Spirituality and the Incarnation in Hans Urs von Balthasar* (Notre Dame: University of Notre Dame Press, 1996).

2. The idea that Jesus "suggests" into being a new personal identity by arousing in us his own desire for the Father has been compellingly explored in the thoughtful work of James Alison, *Raising Abel: The Recovery of the Eschatological Imagination* (New York: Crossroad, 1996) and *The Joy of Being Wrong: Original Sin through Easter Eyes* (New York: Crossroad, 1998). I am much indebted to his fertile insights.

3. Augustine, *The Confessions*, X.27, trans. John K. Ryan (Garden City: Image Books, 1960), 254–255.

4. Rowan Williams, *Resurrection: Interpreting the Easter Gospel* (New York: Pilgrim Press, 1984), 43–44.

5. Simone Weil, *Gravity and Grace*, trans. Emma Craufurd (London: Routledge, 1963), 28.

6. *Ibid.*, 30.

7. John Polkinghorne, *The Faith of a Physicist: Reflections of a Bottom-Up Thinker*, The Gifford Lectures, 1993–1994 (Minneapolis: Fortress Press, 1996), 167.

8. For the brilliant and delightful original, see McCabe, *God Matters*, 123–129, 153–154.

9. *Ibid.*, 127.

10. *Ibid.*, 175.

Resources

Because theology is so often thought of as an academic discipline, it is tempting to approach it as purely a matter of the head. Throughout this book I have suggested that while academic theology has its uses, it must always follow and interpret the church's own encounter with God. In the primary and most important sense theology is something we all do by virtue of our baptism.

Anglicans have a long tradition of holding theology and spirituality, prayer and understanding together in just this way. Among early Anglican theologians, see the writings of Anselm of Canterbury, Aelred of Rievaulx, Julian of Norwich, Lancelot Andrewes, John Donne, George Herbert, and Thomas Traherne. Many of these writers' works are currently available in paperback editions.

∾ Modern and Contemporary Anglican Theologians

John Henry Newman's *Selected Sermons, Prayers, and Devotions* (Vintage, 1999) are especially concerned with the relationship of prayer, belief, and personal holiness, while Evelyn Underhill's *School of Charity: Meditations on the Christian Creed* (Morehouse, 1991) is a beautiful traversal of the essentials of Christian belief from the standpoint of one seeking to pray into the heart of the Christian mysteries. All the works of Austin Farrer exemplify the keenest of intellects hungering for the vision of God, and a good introduction is his *Essential Sermons*, edited by Leslie Houlden (Cowley, 1991). A crucial figure in the contemporary development of this approach to theology is Archbishop Michael Ramsey, whose many works deserve much study. See especially the anthology *To Believe is to Pray: Readings from Michael Ramsey*, edited by James E. Griffiss (Cowley, 1996).

Other writers in this tradition include: Mother Mary Clare, SLG, *Encountering the Depths* (Morehouse, 1981); A. M. Allchin, *Participation in God: A Forgotten Strand in Anglican Tradition* (Morehouse, 1988); John Macquarrie, *Paths in Spirituality* (SCM, 1972); Andrew Louth, *Discerning the Mystery: An Essay on the Nature of Theology* (Oxford, 1983) and *Theology and Spirituality* (Cistercian, 1976); Kenneth Leech, *Experiencing God: Theology and Spirituality* (HarperCollins, 1985); Ellen Charry, *By the Renewing of Your Minds: The Pastoral Function of Christian Doctrine* (Oxford, 1997); Mark A. McIntosh, *Mystical Theology: The Integrity of Spirituality and Theology* (Blackwell, 1998); and Rowan Williams, *A Ray of Darkness: Sermons and Reflections* (Cowley, 1995).

On issues of theology and Anglican identity, see especially Stephen Sykes, *The Integrity of Anglicanism* (Mowbray, 1979) and *Unashamed Anglicanism* (Abingdon, 1995), and Paul Avis, *Anglicanism and the Christian Church* (Fortress, 1989). Alister E. McGrath offers an evangelical perspective in *The Renewal of Anglicanism* (Morehouse, 1993). For a parallel vision, see the invigorating essays in *Living Tradition: Affirming Catholicism in the Anglican Church*, edited by

Jeffrey John (Cowley, 1992). Another collection is *Reclaiming Faith: Essays on Orthodoxy in the Episcopal Church and the Baltimore Declaration*, edited by Ephraim Radner and George R. Sumner (Eerdmans, 1993).

Some useful surveys of Anglican theological concerns include *The Study of Anglicanism*, edited by Stephen Sykes and John Booty (Fortress, 1988); *Theology in Anglicanism*, edited by Arthur Vogel (Morehouse Barlow, 1984); *A New Conversation: Essays on the Future of Theology and the Episcopal Church*, edited by Robert Boak Slocum (Church Publishing, 1999); and *Prayer Book Doctrine: The Teaching of the Episcopal Church based on its Book of Common Prayer*, edited by J. Robert Wright (forthcoming from Church Publishing).

～ One-Volume Surveys of Theology

There are a large number of single-volume surveys, but let me suggest some that combine real insight with clarity and inspiration. The most introductory is C. S. Lewis's three short volumes under the title *Mere Christianity: The Case for Christianity, Christian Behaviour*, and *Beyond Personality* (Macmillan, 1960). More nuanced but still highly accessible is Nicholas Lash's *Believing Three Ways in One God: A Reading of the Apostles' Creed* (Notre Dame, 1993). A remarkable Anglican work covering the central range of Christian theological topics is William Temple's *Christus Veritas* (Macmillan, 1924). Austin Farrer offers a conversational masterpiece in *Saving Belief: A Discussion of Essentials* (Hodder & Stoughton, 1964).

John Polkinghorne examines the creed from the perspective of modern science in his *Faith of a Physicist: Reflections of a Bottom-up Thinker* (Augsburg/Fortress, 1996). For two other readings of the creed, see Karl Barth, *Dogmatics in Outline* (Harper & Row, 1959) and Richard A. Norris, *Understanding the Faith of the Church* (Seabury Press, 1979). Theologian Christos Yannaras offers an Eastern Orthodox perspective in *Elements of Faith: An Introduction to Orthodox Theology* (T & T Clark, 1991). Roman Catholic theologian Elizabeth Johnson has written from a feminist viewpoint in her widely praised work entitled *She Who Is: The Mystery of God in Feminist Theological Discourse* (Crossroad, 1993).

An Anglican writer concerned with the nature and method of theology is Gareth Jones in *Christian Theology: A Brief Introduction* (Polity, 1999). Sometimes theology is written with a verve and relish that reveals the sheer exhilaration of thinking about God, as in the work of Herbert McCabe in *God Matters* (Geoffrey Chapman, 1987). Another creative and original approach is James Alison's *The Joy of Being Wrong: Original Sin through Easter Eyes* (Crossroad, 1998).

∾ Particular Doctrines
The reading gets more advanced here, but rarely impenetrable. Since it would be hopeless to try offering a syllabus of greatest works on each topic of theology from every time and place, I have simply identified a selected number of twentieth-century Anglican writers on some particular questions in theology.

Three classics on the nature of God are William Temple's *Nature, Man and God* (Macmillan, 1934), E. L. Mascall's *He Who Is: A Study in Traditional Theism* (Longmans, 1943), and Dorothy L. Sayers's *The Mind of the Maker* (Harper & Row, 1979). Anglicans continue to contribute vigorously to the contemporary renaissance in trinitarian theology, as in David S. Cunningham's *These Three Are One: The Practice of*

Trinitarian Theology (Blackwell, 1998). Theologian Keith Ward has written a series on particular Christian doctrines in conversation with other world religions, including *Religion and Human Nature* (Clarendon Press, 1998). A classic on the theme of Christian anthropology is David E. Jenkins' *The Glory of Man* (SCM Press, 1967).

Three creative discussions of incarnation and salvation are Frank Weston, *The One Christ: An Enquiry into the Manner of the Incarnation* (Longmans, 1914), R. C. Moberly, *Atonement and Personality* (John Murray, 1917), and L. S. Thornton, *The Incarnate Lord* (Longmans, 1928). Three more recent explorations are Rowan Williams, *Resurrection: Interpreting the Easter Gospel* (Morehouse, 1994), Arthur A. Vogel, *Radical Christianity and the Flesh of Jesus* (Eerdmans, 1995), and John Macquarrie, *Christology Revisited* (Trinity, 1998).

On questions of biblical interpretation and the meaning of Christ, Anglicans are in the debt of theologian Hans Frei, especially his *The Eclipse of the Biblical Narrative* (Yale, 1974), *The Identity of Jesus Christ* (Fortress, 1975), and *Theology and Narrative* (Oxford, 1993).

On the doctrine of the church and its relation to history and culture, see Michael Ramsey's luminous *The Gospel and the Catholic Church* (Cowley, 1990), and more recently, Ephraim Radner, *The End of the Church: A Pneumatology of Christian Division* (Eerdmans, 1998). On the relationship between Christian thought and culture more generally, see Kathryn Tanner, *Theories of Culture: A New Agenda for Theology* (Augsburg/Fortress, 1997). Regarding the goal of Christian life there is the classic by Kenneth Kirk, *The Vision of God* (Longmans, 1931) and more recently,

Anna Williams, *The Ground of Union: Deification in Aquinas and Palamas* (Oxford, 1999).

Finally, a group of Anglican scholars are attempting to place Christian thought in critical dialogue with contemporary postmodern perspectives. As an introduction, see *Radical Orthodoxy: A New Theology*, edited by John Milbank, Catherine Pickstock, and Graham Ward (Routledge, 1999). More complex but enormously stimulating are John Milbank, *The Word Made Strange: Theology, Language, Culture* (Blackwell, 1997) and Catherine Pickstock, *After Writing: On the Liturgical Consummation of Philosophy* (Blackwell, 1998).

Questions for Group Discussion

~ **Chapter One: Mysteries of Faith**

1. In this introductory chapter the author describes theology as "sidling up to these mysteries of faith and peering into their depths," while mystery itself he defines as "the deep dimension of life where meaning dwells." What do you think of this definition of theology? How would you put it in your own words?

2. Throughout this chapter we hear that part of being a Christian and taking part in a community of faith is developing "the habit of theology." In what ways are you a theologian? What are some of the moments in your life that have invited you to think theologically?

~ **Chapter Two: The New Encounter with God**

1. In this chapter we see Jesus through the eyes of the early church and learn how the communities these Christians formed provided new ways for them to relate to one another and to God. In what way has this also been true of your own experience as a member of a church?

2. Christians who are drawn into the communion of love we call the Trinity actually take on a new identity. McIntosh argues that our true sense of self arises out of this common journey with others. Where have you found communities that enabled you to become who you are? Are there particular church rites that have reinforced this sense of a new identity for you, such as baptism or eucharist? How do they do so?

～ Chapter Three: The Splendor of God

1. In *The Mind of the Maker* Dorothy Sayers compares the creativity of the novelist, who creates characters and then must give them their freedom on the page, to the creativity of God in making men and women. What are some of your own experiences of creativity? What have they taught you about the creativity of God?

2. This chapter on creation compares God's creation of the world out of love to our own creation of families and other human communities. In what ways does this ring true? What are our responsibilities to God's creation and our own "creations"?

～ Chapter Four: The Voice of God

1. Revelation shows us who God is. Traditionally Christians have contemplated creation (the Book of Nature) and the Bible (the Book of Scripture) as the two sources of knowledge about God, but today many Christians also demand "facts" and seek after certainty. In what areas do you require certainty about who God is? What proof do you need?

2. In this chapter the author stresses the connection between revelation and personal transformation. Revelation cannot occur in a vacuum; it does not take

place apart from our relationships with God and others. In what ways have your relationships with others revealed something of God?

∿ Chapter Five: The Humanity of God

1. Read through the collect for the Second Sunday after Christmas found on page 214 of *The Book of Common Prayer*. It glorifies God who "wonderfully created, and yet more wonderfully restored, the dignity of human nature." This link between creation and incarnation has always attracted Anglicans, who claim that their faith is deeply incarnational. In what ways do you see this connection in the rites and sacraments of your own church?

2. In this chapter the author says that Jesus did not come to bring us a message, but a person and a relationship. When Jesus appeared to the disciples after the resurrection it was to restore them to a relationship with the Father. What do you think it means to fall out of relationship with God? What does it take to restore something that is broken?

∿ Chapter Six: The Glory of Humanity

1. In this chapter on salvation the author states that human beings have been "so blinded by envy, fear, and violence that the true life of God has become unimaginable." He believes that in the death of Jesus we can see the effects of sin, and in the resurrection "Jesus is able to destroy the lie about death's ultimacy and so pry us loose from its grip." How does this understanding of the death and resurrection of Jesus compare to your own?

2. Describe some occasions on which you were aware of sin being "unmasked." Have there been times when

you experienced what it is like to be caught up in institutional sin, the sin inherent in political, religious, and family systems? Can you name some _institutional_ sins that reveal themselves only through the behavior of individuals?

~ **Chapter Seven: The Drama of the Cosmos**
1. Perhaps the most important teaching of this book is that for Christians who truly seek God, theology and spirituality can never be separated. In other words, we are asked to seek God with both our hearts _and_ our intellects, with love _and_ understanding. In what ways could this understanding lead you to act and pray differently in the future?

2. At the beginning of this book the author tells us that "theology is the working out in disciplined reflection of what happens to us when we accept the call to take up our cross and follow Christ." Each chapter has taken up one of the mysteries of faith: Trinity, creation, revelation, incarnation, salvation, and eschatology. Discuss some of the insights you have gained about these mysteries of faith through your reading of this book.